CONSUMING FAITH

CONSUMING
FAITH

*Integrating Who
We Are with
What We Buy*

TOM BEAUDOIN

SHEED & WARD
Lanham, Chicago, New York, Toronto, and Oxford

Published by Sheed & Ward
An imprint of Rowman & Littlefield Publishers, Inc.
A wholly owned subsidary of The Rowman & Littlefield Publishing Group, Inc.
4501 Forbes Boulevard, Suite 200
Lanham, MD 20706

PO Box 317
Oxford
OX2 9RU, UK

Distributed by National Book Network

All scripture citations in *Consuming Faith* are from the New Revised Standard Version of the Bible.

Library of Congress Cataloging-in-Publication Data

Beaudoin, Tom, 1969–
    Consuming faith : integrating who we are with what we buy / Tom Beaudoin.
        p. cm.
    Includes bibliographical references.
    ISBN 1-58051-138-4
    1. Consumption (Economics)—Religious aspects—Christianity. 2. Brand name products—Religious aspects—Christianity. I. Title.
    BR115.C67 B43 2003
    241'.68—dc22   2003017917

Printed in the United States of America.

♾™ The paper used in this publication meets the minimum requirements of American National Standard for Information Sciences—Permanence of Paper for Printed Library Materials, ANSI/NISO Z39.48-1992.

To Tina

love is God

for God (know not) does love (not does)

whoever

1 John 3:8

CONTENTS

Preface   ix

Acknowledgments   xv

1 Living in a Branded Culture   1

2 A Divine Economy   15

3 Today's Spiritual Discipline: 37
   The Brand Economy

4 Bodies and Branding   61

5 Economic Spirituality: Starting with the Body   77

6 The Challenge of a Maturing   91
   Economic Spirituality

   Appendix: On Reading Scripture   109

   Notes   115

   About the Author   121

PREFACE

"I'm gonna have to check on that."

Lite jazz, then "Mailroom, Jimmy."

"Um," I stalled, conjuring his face from the Midwestern twang of his two-word greeting. He had a mullet and cranked the Allman Brothers, and was one of the few people on earth to whom you would unreservedly loan money or confess besetting sins.

"*Hello*," he semi-drawled. Radio in the background.

"Okay," I continued. "I bought a belt from your company a while back, and I'm just trying to find out where it was made, who made it, that kind of stuff. Somehow I got transferred from a vice president to you in the mail room."

"Can't help you with that one. Sorry," he said, and I wondered if he wondered how normal this conversation was.

"Thanks." And out of patronizing solidarity or Midwestern fellow-feeling, I added "dude." As I hung up, the first few notes of "Black Dog" escaped over the line. Zeppelin. I was close.

This was phone call #6 out of an eventual 43 calls to the headquarters of major corporations. A few weeks earlier, I had pulled out my favorite branded items from my closet. In addition to the $20 black and brown reversible belt from a popular retail outlet, I pulled out two pair of casual and work shoes ($35 and $100), my favorite jeans ($35), and a sport coat I often wore ($150).

I went to the websites of the brands, looking for policies about overseas factory practices and tracking down phone numbers for corporate headquarters. Many companies, I quickly discovered, do not make their full policies available to the public. For most of the rest who do, their policies are written in such legalistic euphemism that it is impossible to know to what they are actually committing themselves. Hard phone time is required, which is how I accidentally met Jimmy.

I cultivated a discriminating appreciation for the diversity of on-hold muzaks as companies often rerouted me up to 15 or more times. I spoke to various managers, middle managers, supervisors, public relations representatives, customer sales representatives, two mail room attendants, and executives. It was evident from the beginning that the run-around was evidence of embarrassment about how their branded products are actually made. Every corporation asked me who I was working for, as if I could only be motivated by allegiance to a communist cause or was moleing for a media exposé. (In my more pious days, I would have replied sunnily, "Jesus!")

The interrogation became like the ritual in Monty Python's *Holy Grail*: "*What* is your name?" "*What* is your quest?" I often tried to mumble something about being concerned, as a person of faith, about human dignity. But having been out-pioused by conservatives and out-justiced by liberals too many times in my life, I gave even that meager statement with hesitant self-consciousness. I'm sure I sounded like I was making it all up, and was really working for Karl Marx.

Many young adults live with the feeling that someone somewhere may be suffering because of the way that their coffee, shoes, clothes, or computers are produced, but many in the middle class are too busy, tired, or already have enough of their own "issues," as they say, to even begin to do anything about it. I was one of them.

I had been doing a lot of writing in coffee shops and had developed an addiction to some particular drinks at a well-known coffee chain. I am not now, nor have I ever been, an economist. But somewhere along the way I read some economic analyses about impoverished coffee farmers in Latin America harvesting coffee for large U.S. corporations. I knew that I was spending nearly $4 a visit for my lattes (easily $1,500 a year), and I was curious about how my coffee shop was spending this money. Having worked on a college newspaper staff, I summoned a mix of shamelessness and tact to phone my way up the corporate hierarchy of this coffee company, eventually getting an interview with one of their vice presidents. I was, perhaps naively, stunned to learn that this company refused to take responsibility for living wages for their coffee farmers through a series of distancing measures, by employing layers of midlevel "independent" operators to relate to farmers. Through a deft business mechanism, they pronounced themselves unaccountable to the workers they depended on the most.

Right around that time, I was giving talks to an auditorium full of Lutheran campus ministers about my first book, *Virtual Faith*. They listened attentively and generously, as only a tradition so steeped in "hearing the word" can do. But after I had spoken for an hour about the ways in which contemporary movies, television, and music influence the spiritual lives of young adults, a spry white-haired cleric with the demeanor of a kindly drill sergeant leapt up from the front row. It was the Rev. Tom Chittick, who was at the time pastor of University Lutheran Church in Cambridge, Massachusetts. Having demonstrated one of the spiritual gifts of Lutheran Christians (rigorous listening), Rev. Chittick was about to show me another one: direct, unvarnished rhetoric. "This is all very interesting," he said, convincingly, "but pop culture is part of a larger economic system. Movies and music and all types of media are all part of buying and selling. What about pop culture as advertisement? What about the economic effects of pop culture on young adults?" My defensive academic strategies instinctively rose up—I immediately started shuffling through various possible ways to dodge the questions that were sounding like accusations. He finished with a flourish: "There is a whole economic analysis missing in your presentation and that we are in serious need of." I had never been so thrown on the defensive at a speaking event. Realizing the apocalyptic nature of the moment, I managed something about him having a good point. Instead of merely making a mental note, I memorized his whole soliloquy.

A few weeks later, back in the safety of my office and away from those truth-telling Lutherans, I wondered if my defensiveness was because Rev. Chittick was being prophetic. Talking about pop culture and spirituality without looking at the role of the economy was like writing about the rain forests without giving any indication that there are actually trees there. That was when I discovered a book by a young Jewish Torontonian journalist, Naomi Klein, called *No Logo*. Klein was beginning to make some of those connections between pop culture and the economy, and the point of contact for her was branding. She showed how brands have come to dominate the visual and mental landscape of North American young adulthood in the last decade and, further, how our enjoyment of brands depends on the exploitation of workers around the world whose working conditions Klein summarized and whom she interviewed. In her remarkably nonmoralizing approach to the influence of corporate branding, and for the audacity of her illegal adventures into overseas sweatshops, I saw in Klein the first plausible candidate for a credible public intellectual from my generation.

With nothing more than an intuition that Klein was right, and a desire as a theologian to bring spiritual questions and analysis to the branding economy (and finding it harder and harder to kick against the goads of my coffee interviews and Chittick's challenge), I knew I had to get educated. I spent the next several years reading anthropological, sociological, and economics accounts of consumer society in general and branding in particular. And the more I looked at my own life, and the lives of my students, I realized that branding was indeed one important point of contact between our economy and pop culture—and one that, I slowly came to see, influences most of us significantly.

These three interruptions inspired me to drop the book I was writing (something much more boring and predictable about Catholic identity), to stall the completion of my doctoral dissertation even further, and to undertake a clothing inventory. I decided to inquire about the conditions under which many of my favorite clothing items and shoes were produced. That's how I met Jimmy. These companies I had been patronizing for many years threw up almost every imaginable firewall, evasion, and euphemism to keep from revealing this information to me. What I learned convinced me that I had to write a book to help me think through my deeply changing sense of spiritual responsibility.

This book begins with a look at how branding works in the lives of the post-1960s generations and why brands have a spiritual significance for all of us. The first chapter lays out the economic landscape in which many young adults live today, in a culture permeated by brand pressures and an economy deeply tied to the fate of young adult workers half a world away. The second chapter looks at aspects of life that are often kept separate, the spiritual and the economic, and finds in a first-century Jewish man, Jesus of Nazareth, a way in which spirituality and economics are part of one full and flourishing life. It is barely an overstatement to say that Christians have spent twenty centuries putting asunder what Jesus had joined.

Next, in chapter 3, I turn back to the brand economy and try to break with commentators who either celebrate it or vilify it, to try to ask if there are deeply religious or spiritual reasons why the brand economy is as persuasive as it is. I try to show that one reason the brand economy "works" is that it brings a similar sort of meaningful order and coherence to people's lives that classic spiritual disciplines once did in the past (and still do for some today). This is not to make apologies for the brand economy, but to show that it is a spiritual force to be reckoned with, and that people are not idiotic dupes of advertisers but soulfully hungry persons looking for a way to bring a sense of meaningful discipline to their lives. Maybe the brand economy and traditional spiritual disciplines have some things to learn from each other.

These old and new disciplines are not just providers of interesting concepts, but affect human bodies—through what we wear, how we pray, and how branded products are made. So chapters 4 and 5 try to figure out how branding effects especially the bodies of those who sew, glue, and stitch our branded products, as well as the insights and dangers of a theology of the body in my own religious tradition, Christianity.

But once we understand the religious allure of branding, the central place of the body (our own and others') for spirituality, and the importance for a maturing spirituality of making good economic choices, what do we actually *do*? The sixth and final chapter offers recommendations for developing your economic spirituality, individually and communally. It is only in everyday living that we allow ourselves to take hold of a more consuming faith, more deeply integrating who we are with what we buy.

ACKNOWLEDGMENTS

In this exploration of economic spirituality in the midst of corporate branding culture, a voyage to a far country buried inside my daily life, I have depended on the wisdom and encouragement of a host of guides.

Many places have provided opportunities for me to test-drive these ideas in the last five years. Among them are: the College Theology Society; Frank J. Lewis Institute at University of San Diego; Seabury-Western Seminary; LaSalle University in Philadelphia; the Archdiocese of Detroit; Assumption University in Windsor, Ontario; Glastonbury Abbey in Hingham, MA; Columbia Theological Seminary in Decatur, GA; the Princeton Theological Seminary Lectures on Youth, Church and Culture; Our Lady of Holy Cross College in New Orleans, LA; the Evangelical Lutheran Church in America Hein-Fry Lectures; Drury University in Springfield, MO; the Presbytery of Baltimore; the New England Episcopal Clergy Conference; the ELCA Nebraska Synod; the United Methodist Church Cal-Pac Conference; the Archdiocese of Los Angeles Religious Education Congress; Hawaiian Islands Ministries; the Episcopal Church Evangelism Conference; the Pastoral Summit; the Lutheran Education

Association; the Massachusetts Institute of Technology Episcopal Chaplaincy; the Pennsylvania ELCA Bishop's Convocation; and Prof. Bill Spohn and Santa Clara University, who through the Bannan Institute provided the occasion for my first academic corralling of these ideas.

A writing retreat at St. John's Abbey in Collegeville, Minnesota, in summer 2002 allowed me to draft a substantial portion of the manuscript. I am very grateful to the monks of St. John's and especially to Fr. Timothy Backous, OSB, for their uniquely Benedictine generosity.

Naomi Klein provided the literary inspiration and Rev. Tom Chittick the spiritual provocation for this book. Jeremy Langford of Sheed & Ward has been a heartily collegial and helpfully critical editor. Martina Verba and Loye Ashton provided helpful commentary on the manuscript. My family has hung by me through all the turbulence and travel of the last several years. My *Incizion* bandmates Loye, David Lopez, and Ralph Guevarez rock. *Myth 2* allowed me to enjoy getting battered by fellow videogame dorks late at night. Kent State remains my American Jerusalem. Rush continues to be my arena-rock religion. Michelle Malone is an inspiring American original who deserves a bigger audience (so: www.michellemalone.com). Karl Rahner, Dietrich Bonhoeffer, and Geddy Lee have charted for me stations on the way to freedom.

Tina, my angel: to you, gratitude for the everydayness of a love supreme.

Good theology, like a good rock bass line, is musical, disclosing the restless and searching *eros* of the author through a melodious percussivity that refers the hearer to their own questing musicality. Wherever my performance is deficient, I may hope that there is such a thing as being helpfully unmusical.

Tom Beaudoin
Boston, Massachusetts
22 June 2003
Feast of Saint Thomas More

CHAPTER 1

LIVING IN A BRANDED CULTURE

I never imagined myself as an activist about the global economy, and indeed "activism" is too strong a word to describe my clothing inventory. But I was in the process of a religious conversion. Just as some of Saint Augustine's key conversional insights were sparked by what he learned from secular philosophers, so my own conversion was catalyzed by a book by the journalist Naomi Klein. Her book *No Logo* examines the way branding has changed everyday life in North America in the last few decades, especially in the lives of the post–Baby Boomer generations.

Klein shows how corporate branding—those labels and insignias and logos of which we are so conscious—influences young adult self-identity to a deep degree today. Whether we see it or not (and whether young adults go along with or rebel against them) brands strongly influence teen and young adult self-understanding.

So many of us identify so strongly with the brands of products we like, that it almost seems natural for us to do so. It is part of being young and middle class today. But Klein showed me that there are specific reasons that brands are so prominent for young adult identity. What I thought was normal and, therefore, harmless is, it turns out, cultural—with benefits and drawbacks for today's young adults as well as those who make our branded products.

According to Klein, in the last several years, corporations have shifted as much or more attention to development of brand *identities* as to improvements in the *products* themselves. In a sense, the brand has become the product; we purchase the brand as much as the branded object. In the words of one corporate report on branding, "performance used to be enough; now personality counts."[1] Or as one senior vice president said, "The brand is the most important asset of the company and its management must be [of] primary concern for top management as well as the board."[2] The shift is summarized most baldly by business authors Al Ries and Laura Ries, who write that "Building your brand on quality is like building your house on sand." Quality "has little to do with [brand] success in the marketplace."[3]

By focusing on branding, companies hope to make their logos into a "personality"—that is, a lifestyle, an image, an identity, or a set of values. Brands should, in the words of one business report, "emote a distinctive persona."[4] This persona will, it is hoped, be taken on with verve by young consumers—whose collective disposable income stretches into the tens of millions of dollars (averaging over $100 a week per sixteen-year-old).[5]

To a large extent, corporations have been successful, even among the very young. Journalist Alissa Quart recounts the boast of one corporate marketer who announced to an advertising conference that "the average ten-year-old has memorized from three hundred to four hundred brands. Ninety-two percent of kids request brand-specific products."[6]

And growing into adulthood under corporate branding means that to a remarkable degree, young adults come to know themselves and are known by peers in and through relationships to brands.

Often, however, there is an intergenerational disconnect about the power of branding. Older adults have trouble understanding its power, and younger adults have difficulty explaining its attraction. As Klein—herself a child of the '70s and '80s—writes, for younger generations, the search for self [has] always been shaped by marketing hype, whether or not [we] believed it or defined [our]selves against it. This is a side effect of brand expansion that is far more difficult to track and quantify than the branding of culture and city spaces. This loss of space happens inside the individual; it is a colonization not of physical space but of mental space.[7]

Contemporary philosophers emphasize that we all "perform" our identity. What they mean is that through speech patterns, gestures, clothing styles, and various verbal and nonverbal cues, we creatively put together who we are, as much as who we are is "given" to us naturally. We all have different personae that we "perform" or display, and those cues—verbal and nonverbal, clothing and makeup and energy and rhythm—are all part of the freedom we have to create who we are in different domains of our lives.

For those of us who live deeply immersed in the branding economy, we make an identity for ourselves, and an identity is made for us, by our relationships to consumer goods: what and how we own, when and why we wear. Clothes and other branded products do "identity work" for us, transmitting messages about ourselves to ourselves and others. Never before have young generations had to contend with such an intensive culture of corporations who want to sponsor this identity work for us. Just as businesses vie to win official sponsorship of the Olympics and Super Bowl, companies compete to be the corporate sponsors of young adult life. Our images of our successful and confident selves are often "brought to you by. . . ."

Around the time I was calling those companies who had sponsored my young adult identity, I was curious about whether my undergraduate students also related to brands as Klein and I (two 30-somethings) had. They were, after all, born a full decade or more after us.

So one day in class I asked these mostly middle class (and less than 20 percent minority) students to imagine their successful selves. With what brands, I continued, do you picture yourselves associating?

I realized later that at that moment there were no puzzled looks or confused faces—something that as a teacher I would hopefully notice immediately. Few if any of my students heard this as a strange question.

Passing around a few pieces of paper, I asked them to list those brands. They generated well over one hundred of them (which, in my attempt to avoid serving as an inadvertent steward of these brands, I will not list here).

When I talked individually with many of them later, I realized that each student could describe the image or lifestyle associated with the brands they liked. Some students preferred one baggy, unadorned brand, for example, because their clothes resembled the funky, blue-collar attire of a service station attendant, allowing them to step away from their middle-class suburban look. Others liked this brand because certain gangs were rumored to wear it and so it helped students affect a tough, streetwise persona. Sometimes a certain star or model was associated with a brand, and students said that wearing that brand associated them with that star's image or values.

As any teacher today may observe, my male students were no less immersed in brand culture than my female students. Some researchers are discovering that young men are as unabashed partakers in the branded clothing culture as women. Summarizing data on men's fading self-consciousness about being a clothes horse, *New York Times* reporter Ruth La Ferla reported on young men's "heightened brand awareness," observing that

> for a new breed of teenage boys and young men, clothes shopping, once a chore, is now a pleasurable pastime, a form of recreation, self-expression, even fulfillment, motivations rarely acknowledged in their fathers' day, but that young men now share with female contemporaries.[8]

This exercise did not make me condescend to my students, because in addition to being a walking billboard for the brands whose products I pulled out of my closet, I confess to having worn certain black tennis shoes because they were favored by Geddy Lee, singer-bassist for the rock group Rush (who I have hyperidolized since 1981). I hoped to capture his suburban white-boy groove by wearing them.

BRANDING AND SPIRITUAL POWER

I now associate those black sneakers with an offbeat, casually anti-institutional smartness. My branded sandals, in a similar manner, signify an earthy, progressive sensibility. On one level, I feel silly even writing about elevating a sneaker or sandal to such status. No object transmits meaning without humans investing it with emotional meaning individually and socially—what psychologists call "cathecting" objects.

Yet there is also spiritual power in these branded objects. Understanding ourselves as humans seems unavoidably indirect. We always must go through a third party. Individually and communally, we only come to know who we are in and through "mediations"—other people, objects, symbols, language. Theological language makes this everyday reality sound elegant: the world is the potential sacrament of human becoming.

The world of our products is thus spiritually volatile. Through our relation to products we become more faithful, hopeful and loving—or more covetous and self-enclosed.

Branding always trades on this spiritual power of worldly goods. But the corporate brander must condense and abbreviate that spiritual power: the logo must communicate meaning quickly, before our eyes search elsewhere for spiritual direction, for objects or materials through which we can define and express who we are becoming. Philosopher Mark C. Taylor recognized that "The effectiveness of the logo depends upon its transparency and the immediacy of its meaning. The logo is designed to be grasped in an instant."[9]

Branding is a particularly powerful force for adolescents and young adults, who are in critical stages of their lives, piecing together adult identities, trying on different ways of being, different self-images. From one's early teens into one's thirties, discovering and creating a coherent identity with which one can really live is a major project. More than ever, we use corporate brands to experiment with these identities—and corporate brands use us. Business literature shows that corporations know this, and it influences their branding strategies. They know that if they can enter into people's identity work before adolescence, then once those awkward teenage years start, teens will be more likely to look to brands for an acceptable identity. And corporations know that if young adults get settled into certain brands through which they declare their self-identity, then those brands will be more likely a part of that person's identity ensemble as they move into adulthood and middle age.

BRANDING AND CORPORATE POWER

For corporations, the intensive focus on branding offers other advantages. It allows a company to roll out new products that will find a ready market because they fall under the same brand umbrella. How many well-branded pop musicians today introduce not only CDs but concert shirts, playing cards, pay-for-access web sites, videos and DVDs, jackets, jewelry, and even credit cards? On those rare occasions that I hear a fresh new rock band that startles me out of '80s nostalgia, I look up these new bands on the Internet. Every single one of these bands in the last several years has debuted fully branded, with a cool logo, street team gear, postcards, clothing, bobble-head dolls, and other items. Apart from new corporate entities like rock bands, even decades-old large corporate luxury liners invent many new products that are all carefully tethered to the logo of the mother ship.

When was the last time you watched a new television show or mainstream movie that did not showcase, however subtly, certain brands? Cross-promotion, of course, becomes much easier when brands get visibly placed in movies, music videos, and other forms of entertainment. This cross-promotion often tries to homogenize middle class life. Today's teens will, in the words of one ad agency's study of over 27,000 teens in over 45 countries, "get up in the morning, put on their [brand A] and [brand B], grab their caps, backpacks, and [brand C] personal CD players, and head for school." This branded world, found this study, is connected most significantly by television, especially MTV, watched by 85 percent of those surveyed.[10]

Klein wryly observes that "Global teens watch so much MTV per day that the only equivalent shared cultural experience among adults occurs during an outbreak of war when all eyes are focused on the same CNN images."[11]

Many cable shows help promote brands. The success of one cable show with young women in their twenties and thirties, for example, spawned several parties and fashion shows to promote brands of bags, shoes, and hair products seen on the show. At one event, one hair product company

> had fashionably dressed sales people cruising the bars handing out red [brand deleted] hair color to patrons who said they identified best with the . . . redhead . . . and [brand excised] to the . . . blondes . . . in the crowd. [The cable channel] is keenly aware of that connection, and the show's official Web site has links to stores that sell fashion items featured on the show.[12]

Because I had thought that this show was only an American phenomenon, I was surprised to learn that these cross-promotional tours took place in Thailand and the Philippines.

The biggest advantage for corporations is that the identity associated with the brand becomes more important than the quality of the product itself. This allows companies to produce cheaper and cheaper products under the same brand image, because people are buying the cachet, image, or identity associated with the brand as much as—or more than—the quality of the product itself. Indeed, as economist Juliet Schor reports in *The Overspent American*, many studies indicate that when brand labels are removed, consumers cannot tell the difference in quality between different jeans, perfumes, and other commonly branded goods.

All of these advantages reveal a staggering aggregation of international corporate power in recent years. Many of our branded products come from Indonesia, China, Taiwan, South Korea, Mexico, Vietnam, the Philippines, and elsewhere. These are not mere startups; such transnational corporations control a disproportionate amount of the world's assets. But instead of making world-historical waggings with my index finger at this power, let me come back to my personal relationship to our modern-day Goliaths, and dozens of annoying phone calls.

UNMASKING THE BRANDS

Let me take you back to the story I began in the preface. Like other semi-informed consumers, I had heard about the sweatshop woes of major tennis shoe companies and celebrity-owned brands. Some of my first-year college students even told me they learned in high school to avoid buying Brand X or Y because of labor concerns. But I never had the guts or occasion to connect all this to my *personal* economy; I was finally doing it by trying to figure out how several of my favorite branded products were actually made.

Six months of leaving unreturned messages, getting transferred back and forth between the same people, being put on hold for interminable amounts of time often followed by "accidental" disconnection, arguing with people who had little influence and even less real knowledge, pursuing false numbers, being referred to evaluations of factory conditions by "inspectors" who were employed by the companies themselves, wading through public relations fogspeak, and then consulting watchdog groups who had some data on these companies—after all this, finally some clear patterns were emerging.

With one exception, none of these companies, bearers of the brands I had come to trust, was proud, forthcoming, or transparent about its labor practices outside the United States. Almost all of them employed young adults, usually young women, in their factories— located in Mexico, the Philippines, Indonesia, and China. (Most companies would not reveal the exact location of their factories.) From what I could dig up, these young women worked 50–60 hours a week, sometimes more. At most, they made the minimum wage, which, as far as I could determine for the countries in which these factories were located, was never anywhere near a living wage. (A living wage is enough to guarantee someone access to the necessities of a dignified life; difficult to calculate, it is nonetheless distinct from a mere "minimum" wage. And it is almost as rare in the United States as it is in the Philippines.)

Most galling to me was that these companies I had been patronizing for many years, companies into whom I had poured thousands of dollars of my disposable income and enormous cathective reserves of my trust, and whom I probably would otherwise have supported the rest of my life, threw up almost every imaginable firewall, evasion, and euphemism to keep from revealing even this minimal information to me.

After six months, I had only enough data to fill up one page of notebook paper, but it was the most outrageous and damning paper I had ever held in my hands.

Only then did I begin to think about the double function of the logo or brand. Not only must it instantaneously conjure up a "personality" with which consumers can identify, it must also draw our attention away from *how* it was produced. The brand both reveals and conceals, a blindfolding embrace.

THE IMPACT OF GLOBALIZATION

The fact that the brands with which we have relationships are made in all corners of the world is one important sign of our times. This intercontinental expansion of most national economies in the last few decades has been studied by many economists and sociologists under a title that evokes praise and condemnation: globalization. But globalization also elicits much confusion. Although I had been personally involved in globalization from the time I first purchased or consumed any product made overseas, I had only begun to wonder what globalization meant when I undertook my clothing inventory.

I soon discovered that the literature on globalization is growing just as quickly as the world is shrinking. Indeed, the notion of a shrinking world is central to globalization. Sociologist Malcolm Waters suggests that globalization has two basic aspects. First, there is an accelerated interconnectedness and interdependence among individuals, societies, and cultures of the world. Peoples of the world depend on each other more than ever, from politics to economics to culture. Waters gives the example of Australian sheep shearers, whose economic security is affected by global forces beyond their control:

> by trends in Japanese fashions, the "Millennium" round of WTO negotiations, [or] the cost of synthetic fibres which is in turn determined by

the price of oil, which might in turn be determined by American military intervention in the Persian Gulf, and the extent to which the Australian government accepts prevailing global ideologies of marketization and privatization.[13]

The second aspect of globalization for Waters is that a "consciousness of the global whole" is increasingly present among peoples of the world.[14] He means that we are more conscious than ever, in our everyday lives, of the reality of people who live lives every bit as important and meaningful as our own but in very different cultural, political and economic contexts. Global media and technology are largely responsible for this. For example, I received email from students who were involved in the Tianenman Square massacre in 1989 while it was happening. My "consciousness of the global whole" was forever changed by knowing that students my age were investing their lives not in careerism or cable television but in defense of their basic human rights.

This second aspect is also evident in the changing consciousness of young generations with regard to religion and spirituality. For example, many young Catholics today believe that Catholicism is not necessarily a more direct route to heaven than any other major religion.[15] This dramatic change in belief away from "no salvation outside the Church" is certainly influenced by the religious pluralism that younger generations have witnessed through 24-hour news, the Internet, television, and other electronic global media.

It was striking that for many years the Dalai Lama has been second only to the bishop of Rome as an object of spiritual curiosity. Respecting both these figures not only illustrates a "consciousness of the global whole" made possible by technology, but also has a democratizing effect on who many young Catholic Christians think they will be seeing in heaven—Jews, Muslims, Hindus, and Buddhists . . . and Protestant Christians, too.

Educator Sharon Parks has recently argued that the most salient cultural factor in the formation of the imagination of young adults today is globalization.[16] We have before us the first generation of emerging adults, living what is the most critical adult stage of their life, coming to maturity within a global culture. In her book *Big Questions, Worthy Dreams,* Parks tells the revealing story of a young adult from the United States doing volunteer work in Nicaragua. He related that local youth asked the American volunteers for "*memorias,* gifts of remembrance, otherwise, they threatened, they would not remember us." What one Nicaraguan young man wanted most of all from his U.S. acquaintance was the branded cap that the volunteer was wearing. "My refusal to give it to him," he reports, "hurt our friendship."[17] The logo on the cap had become a global, cross-cultural symbol for youth identity. His local Nicaraguan culture had been relativized by the brand symbol, probably through the media.

BRANDS AND SPIRITUAL INTEGRITY

Where is faith in all of this?

Specifically for me, someone born into Christianity yet trying to become a Christian, what is my responsibility for the economy? Does God care about how I use my resources? Should economic concerns be important to Christian spirituality, secondary to it, or, finally, a matter of indifference? In short, how deeply ought I integrate who I am in faith with what I buy?

The remaining chapters trace the path of spiritual and theological discovery I have taken in trying to answer these questions. In turning for guidance to the "mission statements" of my faith tradition, the Christian gospels, I realized that they present a vision of relating to the economy that is so shockingly at odds with how Christians actually live that I am left wondering how it is that I say I belong to the same religion as those who wrote the Christian scriptures.

No one had ever told me before that Jesus was God's economist.

CHAPTER 2

A DIVINE ECONOMY

Economists are frequently in the news. Our economy is so volatile, with the middle classes more deeply embroiled in the vagaries of stock market investments, the expenditures of health care plans, and the politics of retirement, that our culture has invested economists with prophetic authority to read the monetary signs of the times. Because the great middle now senses the tenuousness of its position—one parent suddenly out of work now means radical readjustment for many families—we turn to specialists in the circulation of capital to find out how the flow is going and how to keep it flowing.

Economists are now regular commentators on most news programs, and economics (or its sister disciplines, business and management) is a popular major for a wide range of students on many campuses. (In the 1980s, I remember only Young Republicans wanting to major in Econ. Now even many progressive students of mine want to master it, due to their interest in the environment, globalization, business ethics, or simply anxiety about securing a stable future.)

What is it that all these scholars and students of economics are studying? It may come as a surprise that the definitions of an economist are as plural and controversial as definitions of a citizen, a person of faith, or even a theologian. While economists wrangle over the meaning of their vocation, I prefer to look at how economists function in their communities: an economist is someone who advocates for a particular distribution of goods or resources in a community.

We all live in a world of limited goods. How should communities decide who is worthy of what? What should interest rates be? How do people decide between competing products? What is a minimum wage? What is poverty? Even the most *descriptive* economist is always also *prescribing* a particular distribution of resources in and for a given community.

On its face, the task of the economist and the call of the person of faith may seem very different vocations. But, in fact, they strongly overlap.

SORTING OUT "SPIRITUALITY"

One of the most common ways for people of faith to describe themselves today is as "spiritual" persons (as distinct from "religious"). Someone's "spirituality" may be their way of talking about faith in a deity, in nature, in a particular value, or in themselves. However the faith to which this spirituality refers is described, of course, there is no person *without* faith in something or someone.

The fact of radically diverse spiritualities testifies to the seriousness (sometimes through irreverence) with which people take their quests to discover the significance of their lives, to honor and interpret their deepest passions. Any theologian who ignores—or too quickly simplifies—these diverse practical spiritualities has been disqualified from contemporary relevance. And yet if "spirituality" can mean potentially anything, it means nothing. We each have to risk defining our spirituality and defending it publicly, and I too have certain biases about what spirituality is. These biases have been informed by my Christian tradition, and they have also shaped my understanding of that tradition.

Our contemporary passion for spirituality wants to distinguish itself from religion. This seems obvious when spirituality is defined as experiential (as opposed to, say, juridical), interior (versus external or doctrinal), individual (as opposed to institutional), freeing and trust-worthy (neither restrictive nor suspect), pure (not sinful), and a con-nector between religions (as opposed to a wall between them). Today's understanding of spirituality enables people of various reli-gious traditions—and none at all—to respect each other's "journey" of faith. It gives a common faith language to the recovering addict and the gym junkie, the gang member and the politician, the passionate faith practitioner and the indifferent secularist.

This taste for spirituality is rightly cautious about confusing God (or a Higher Power) with human-made structures. Those human-made structures—whether necessary or unnecessary—are usually now called "religion." At the same time, this common approach to spirituality can veer very close to narcissism, the American religion of self-reliance. This happens when each of us uses our "spirituality" to consider ourselves the sole authority on all matters of truth. We veer this direction when we begin to convince ourselves that we have no obligations to the relationships, communities, and traditions that helped make us who we are as individuals.

So I want to take our contemporary turn to spirituality seriously. I want to dignify the importance of coming to truth for oneself as an adult, distinct from religious institutions. And yet I want to avoid a false sense of independence in the process, replacing a smothering concept of God or religion with a godlike concept of the individual that smothers all relationships, that denies our essential dependence on others (from our mothers to our friends, significant others, and our religious and civic associations).

We can navigate these treacherous waters if we think of spirituality as a relationship with the mysterious and gracious power that sustains us, a power that we ourselves did not create and that we cannot con-trol. Spirituality thus starts and ends not with ethereal doctrines, but with our experiences of everyday life, especially the experience of our relationships.

We all experience ourselves as able to act in relation to others under a power we do not control—a power to go "beyond" ourselves in friendship and forgiveness, a power to obey our conscience even at great personal cost, a power to release ourselves to hope in otherwise hopeless situations. Because this reality is a *force* in our lives, I call it a *power*. Because this power is *available* to everyone irrespective of status, I call it *gracious*. Because this gracious power is *never captured* or plumbed by our attempts to name it, even to name it God, I call this gracious power *mysterious*.

The person deserving of the name "spiritual," then, is one who is growing in relationship with that mysterious and gracious power that bears us up, that animates, suffuses, and orients every person's life. This understanding of spirituality does not equate "spirituality" and "religion." Yet it also does not turn the individual into a solitary ghost, without deeply relational material needs. The spiritual person is thus a responsible person—in relationship to the mysterious and gracious Other and, importantly, to others who have tutored us in that relationship.

ECONOMIC SPIRITUALITY

How often do most of us think of economics when we think of our spirituality? And yet, if you are with me this far, it is hard to avoid the conclusion that spirituality and economics have a lot to do with each other. To avoid this is to attempt to keep our spirituality restricted and stagnant—something that our contemporary passion for spirituality quite rightly intends to avoid.

We can all be spiritual in the sense I have described. So, too, are we all economists in the sense described earlier: we all think and act in ways that advocate particular distributions of resources in our communities. (We all buy this and not that; we all patronize certain institutions and not others; we accept certain wages or pay certain wages.) All of our economic actions manifest the implicit distribution of resources for which we advocate. (For example, many of us implicitly advocate that professional athletes should make hundreds of times more than public school teachers, or that our babysitters' income need not be shared with the government through taxes—though we rarely formulate these convictions as our own "economic positions.")

Here is the rub: the distribution of resources for which you advocate is *necessarily* anchored in something. But in what? I propose that it should be anchored in our spirituality.

If you consider it, our spirituality always has an economic dimension: the distribution of resources encourages or discourages people from living in fidelity to the Other and others. Further, living in relation to the mysterious and gracious power must influence how we think resources should be used and distributed.

And likewise, our economics always has a spiritual dimension: every advocacy for a distribution of resources is a manifestation of that to which one is accountable. In every economic activity, we are stating who or what we stand for.

There could be such a thing, then, as an economic spirituality, in short, a process of integrating who we are with what we buy. This is not my own idle speculation or ivory tower theologizing. I learned it from the Jesus of the New Testament, whom for Christians I understand to be God's economist.

GOD'S ECONOMIST

The fact that there are so many Christians (including, too often, me) who think that spirituality is separate from economics is a measure of just how unusual and potentially fresh Jesus' own example is.

One of the most fascinating and underacknowledged aspects of Jesus' life is his preaching of an economic spirituality, an integration of who persons are with how they use their resources. His economic spirituality cannot be reduced to an autonomous "spirituality," on the one hand, and a concern for "economics," on the other, as if heaven and earth are radically separate realms. I believe that people of any faith can learn from Jesus in this regard, but those who are trying to become Christians have a unique obligation to do so.

Our sense of economics and spirituality are both present in Jesus, but as united without separation or confusion. And in living this economic spirituality, he shows what is possible for all persons, what the gracious and mysterious, intimate power he names "Abba, Father" expects of all persons.

For Jesus, humans become themselves by accepting their relationship to God, and that acceptance is manifest by a transfigured distribution of their resources. This is ultimately a fundamentally freeing, and thus saving, message. Therefore, Jesus is rightly called "savior" by Christians—not because he fulfilled prophecy X, Y, or Z, not because of his miracles, not because he "descended" from heaven, but because he is God's economist, revealing what an acceptance of relationship with divine power looks like. Being faithful to God is always manifest practically in a transfigured distribution of resources.

Jesus' economic spirituality is strikingly simple, though far from simplistic. First, he teaches that all resources are ultimately God's. Though humans may come into wealth or goods, and may even create their own store of resources, it is God who is first and last Creator. Anyone who acts as though they have created all of their own "wealth" has put themselves in place of God. Many of us have perhaps experienced the subtle tyrannies of the omnipotent strivings of those who imagine that they breathed all their goods into being.

Second, Jesus teaches that one's resources are to be used for the good of all. This does not mean frivolously throwing money, food, ideas or time in all directions at once. Instead, Jesus continually privileges those who are on the margins of power and social acceptability. It is to the increased livelihood of these persons that one can look when wondering how to use one's resources for the good of others. Jesus' friends, who were certainly not in a position to influence Roman policy in this regard, still practiced this aspect of economic spirituality among themselves, sharing their resources among each other and with the poor (Acts 2:44–45).

Paul, the famous disciple of Jesus, made this economic spirituality important in his own teaching. This first Christian theologian is too often today simplistically imagined as the Apostle of Faith Over Works, or reduced to The Sexual Policeman. His concerns were much broader, however. He personally oversaw a collection for poor associates in Jerusalem, and he was very concerned to see that wealthy members of the community did not take more than they needed at early eucharistic meals (2 Corinthians 8–9, 1 Corinthians 11).

Paul is also sometimes made The Theorist of Spiritual Gifts, for his well-known ruminations on what the gifts of the Spirit are and how they should be used (1 Corinthians 12). But I now wonder whether even these influential teachings of Paul were rooted in part in his economic spirituality. Just as Jesus encourages the use of material resources for the good of all, so Paul comes to the conviction that spiritual gifts are not for private enrichment alone, but, finally, for "the common good" (1 Corinthians 12:7). This famous spiritual doctrine may indeed have been influenced by Jesus' economic teaching and was certainly a heritage of their shared Jewish identity.

Jesus is most clearly God's economist when he talks about life's big questions, such as the sense God makes of human life. When Jesus talks explicitly about God's final judgment on our lives—which he rarely does—he continually refers not to sexual issues; not to proper deference to a pastor, bishop, or pope; not to the inerrancy of scripture; not to membership in a church; not to himself-as-my-personal-Lord-and-savior; not to right ritual. He continually refers to economic spirituality. Jesus clearly made economic spirituality in everyday life the ultimate expression of faithfulness to God.

EVERYDAY ECONOMICS
AND GOD'S "JUDGMENT"

Because there is much misunderstanding about the language of "God's judgment" today, it is worth exploring a bit further—even allowing it to shock us as if for the first time. What is striking about Christian scripture's language about God's judgment and the afterlife is that the Bible frequently talks about economic spirituality in the context of the final, definitive meaning of our lives. It signals this final meaning through language about the afterlife: heaven, Hades, God's final judgment.

However the early Christians interpreted this language, educated Christians today cannot worship God with their minds by believing in a heaven that is somewhere "up there," a rainbowed place where life will continue more or less like it does here, except in great happiness, perhaps with continual festivals of family and friends. Neither can we believe in a hell that is somewhere "down there," a place where flames literally burn souls in an agonizing punishment that goes on without end. If time, and our freedom, is really completed for us at the moment of our death, nothing like our temporal experience "goes on."

I believe that the *afterlife* and *judgment* language of the New Testament are the first century's language for a life-defining experience that we all will have sooner or later. To understand the experience to which this scriptural language refers, we must today use somewhat abstract, existential language so as not to take the Christian scriptural images too literally. In turning to this existential interpretation of the scripture, I have learned a great deal from the Catholic theologian Karl Rahner, whose perspective infuses my work here.

"Judgment" and "afterlife" refer to the "summing up" of our lives, the coming to fulfillment of who we have been in our freedom. That is, "final judgment" images refer to an experience of absolute confrontation with our own life of relationships, of taking a final and complete responsibility for who we have become—to the degree that we have been free to live in relation to God, others, the world, and ourselves. To embrace our history of grace and sin as *ours*. To use the language of contemporary 12-step programs, "final judgment" language refers to a final "fearless and searching inventory" of how we have used our freedom.

To be able to accept ourselves completely and finally, including our guilt, in a final surrender of ourselves into God's holy and forgiving mysterious incomprehensibility—*that* is "ascent" to "heaven." So long as we are unwilling to take final responsibility for who we have freely become, to confront and accept what we have made of our free relationships to ourselves and others—*that* is "descent" into "hell." To "face God" in judgment is to face our history of relating to God in our earthly lives: to accept or reject what we have made of our own relationships.

To honor the spiritually essential nature of relationships in our life, I believe that in death we will experience ourselves somehow— a way no one can describe—as the sum of our relationships. Who we have become in and through others will remain permanently a part of us. How I loved God in how I used my resources in loving my family, my friends, my students, the makers of my clothes, my pets, the natural world, will speak a final, permanent, and eternal word to me, as if the web of relationships that *is* my life will be restored to my final self-understanding, and if I can know, love, and accept that this is who I have become, allow it to be fully present to myself and so to God's healing immediacy that has always and will continue to bear me up, I will then know what immersive participation in God is as the magnification of my life becomes the moment of my fundamental option for or against this uncontrollable and inscrutable mystery which will then dissolve even the name "God" until at last happens a finally reconciling and all-encompassing "peace be with you."

LAZARUS AND GOD'S ECONOMY

One of the clearest "photographs" of Jesus' economic spirituality is his story about Lazarus and the rich man (Luke 16:19–31). Pondering this disturbing story, for Christians anyway, gives some indication of how Jesus imagines a more God-shaped economy. I will paste in this famous story (some readers will have memorized it from over-familiarity, and some will be encountering it for the first time), and after each passage I will attempt to savor the economic spirituality spilling out of this gospel text like so many treasures flowing out the side of a piñata. After considering Lazarus, we will more briefly consider other economic references in the Christian scripture.

You may want first to read all the italicized passages together, as one story, or to simply read the translation in your own Bible. I encourage you to dwell on each section of the scripture, mining it for yourself, comparing your insights to my own.

[19] *Jesus said, There was a rich man who was dressed in purple and fine linen and who feasted sumptuously every day.*

The mention of "purple" immediately stands out as one of the few adjectives of color in the New Testament. Such a hue of throb and throne introduces the ironic tone suffusing this story, for purple alludes to Jesus' poverty. The poor and ironic king Jesus fits into the purple (see Mark 15:17) and provides a contrast to the rich man.

Moreover, irony itself is dressed in "fine linen" here, for in Revelation 19:8, "fine linen" refers to the "righteous deeds of the saints." So we may read this "fine linen" as a reference to the deeds with which the rich man clothes himself.

As if to unite these two allusions, in earlier biblical history, Moses took up an offering of "purple" and "fine linen" (Exodus 25:4). There, God asks for the offering "from all whose hearts prompt them to give." Luke's irony is blessedly understated.

[20] *And at his gate lay a poor man named Lazarus, covered with sores,*

It is interesting that the poor man is named while the rich man is not, as if Lazarus' name is given because it is his only possession.

There is a strong contrast in how they present themselves. The rich man decorated with delicate clothing, and Lazarus decorated with injury or disease. The text murmurs the question: Who is the one who is really ill?

Jesus' presence lurks beneath these lines. In him the rich and poor man find their reference, for he, as Luke knows, was "covered with sores" by his flogging and scourging, and also "dressed in purple" by Roman soldiers. Before two verses have transpired, these verses give an economic shading to the narratives of his passion.

The gate stands forth as the symbol of the passage between the two men, signifying movement, access, traffic. Lazarus, if he moves, moves surely in pain. The rich man presumably moves more easily so as to "feast sumptuously every day." Yet we hear the gate neither creak nor swing. In being content to mind the latch, the rich man fashions an economic chasm between them, a social chasm. A chasmed relationship.

[21] *who longed to satisfy his hunger with what fell from the rich man's table; even the dogs would come and lick his sores.*

The dogs—a strange detail. They are more satisfied than Lazarus; they lick, he hungers. The dogs show more awareness of Lazarus than does the rich man. Are they the rich man's dogs, come through the gate? Are they neighborhood strays, using this sad sack of a man, or comforting him?

Lazarus' dignity has been reduced to living literally like a dog. Scripture elsewhere alludes to the animals that eat what falls from the table as dogs (Matthew 15:27, Mark 7:28). It is as if, prompted by the recollection that Lazarus was reduced to living with dogs, Luke suddenly remembered a neglected detail: "even the dogs."

[22] *The poor man died and was carried away by the angels to be with Abraham. The rich man also died and was buried.*

Without drama, Lazarus dies, apparently at the gate. The rich man's end takes place in a similarly unremarkable manner: he "also died."

The rich man is buried, perhaps in his purple and fine linen. Lazarus has no burial.

This poor man who could not cross the gate to satisfy his hunger now crashes the gate separating him from Abraham, the "friend of God" (James 2:23). We do not know enough about Lazarus to know why God threw open the gate to Abraham for him, though perhaps like Abraham, and like many locked out of a satisfied hunger, it was the fundamental trust present in patient longsuffering, "believing God" (Genesis 15:6).

The unintentional rhyme in one English translation suggests that this passage tells of the spiritual consequences of gluttony: "the poor man was carried . . . the rich man was buried."

[23] *In Hades, where he was being tormented, he looked up and saw Abraham far away with Lazarus by his side.*

We do not know exactly why or how the rich man is being tormented. Since he seems to have self-awareness, perhaps he is being tormented by his own remorse over the free disposition of his life in which he succumbed to a greedy indifference. This is the first time in the story that the rich man actually sees Lazarus, and indeed Lazarus stands, and we see that this associate of the dogs is also human.

Spatially, the rich man has gone from being "above" at table, to being "below" Lazarus, "looking up."

[24] *He called out, "Father Abraham, have mercy on me, and send Lazarus to dip the tip of his finger in water and cool my tongue; for I am in agony in these flames."*

We now learn that the rich man must have known Lazarus in life, as he addresses him by name here, without prompting. He cannot claim to have been blind to this man's existence. And now he begs for Lazarus to bring water, that is, now the rich man pleads for a gate to swing his own way.

As Lazarus once hungered, now the rich man thirsts. We also learn that his torment is from the flames, though we do not know where the flames come from or what they mean. The rich man is learning that the time for giving cold water to the thirsty is in life, not after death (Matthew 10:42).

Notice how the rich man's appeal for mercy is not "directly" to God, but to another "person," Abraham. Just as the appeal for mercy is addressed to a human, in hope of salvation, so too is economic generosity a matter entirely directed to and from other beings in hope of salvation (Luke 18:18–25; Matthew 25). God works in and through humans. By our relations with each other (including those "at our gate"), we save each other or condemn ourselves.

[25] *But Abraham said, "Child, remember that during your lifetime you received your good things; and Lazarus in like manner evil things; but now he is comforted here, and you are in agony."*

Abraham directs the rich man's attention to the utterly singular arena in which we become who we will be for eternity: "your lifetime." Unlike other religions or philosophies, Abraham speaks in the singular, not the plural. We have one life with which to make an only life.

Even while reciting this most revelatory and elementary claim on existence, Abraham's voice catches. Knowing he is powerless to change the decisive character of the during-your-lifetime, still he tenderly addresses the rich man as "child."

Shall we say here that what seems ephemeral during-our-lifetime has eternal significance, or instead that what is of genuine importance during-our-lifetime has eternal significance? Both. For the rich man's relationship to purple, to fine linen, to feasting sumptuously every day, and to the gate are the materials, in time and history, from which his eternity is fashioned. He potters them as the clay of his becoming.

[26] *Besides all this, between you and us a great chasm has been fixed, so that those who might want to pass from here to you cannot do so, and no one can cross from there to us."*

The chasm hollowed out in freedom and in economic history by the rich man's continual refusal of the gate, has now become finally his own. That into which he pitched his freedom has become his final identity.

(Shall we blame God for this? We could not even consider blaming God for this gift of freedom if we had not already fundamentally accepted it.)

Gate has become chasm. The gate to Lazarus, it turns out, was his gate to heaven. Had he realized it "during [his] lifetime," he could have proclaimed with Jacob, "How awesome is this place! This is none other than the house of God, and this is the gate of heaven" (Genesis 28:17).

Jacob understood that our gates to God are not only secret or unintelligible. "Surely the Lord is in *this* place—and I did not know it" (Genesis 28:16b).

[27–28] *He said, "Then, father, I beg you to send him to my father's house—for I have five brothers—that he may warn them, so that they will not also come into this place of torment."*

On the one hand, the rich man has grown in concern for others, wanting to warn his family of the decisive spiritual importance of economic spirituality.

On the other hand, he has not truly confronted himself on this matter. Even after death, he is still seeking to use Lazarus, to ignore his real presence, to protect his own family. To confront Lazarus would be to confront himself. Better to send Lazarus on a mission to save souls—not the last time this strategy will be used.

Luke's irony resurfaces. The rich man refers to "my father's house," which elsewhere means the temple in particular or God's expansive embrace in general (Luke 2:49; John 14:2). In this regard, the rich man has not *five* brothers. His brothers are all Jewish people, or all people. Again, through Luke's irony, the rich man wants to narrow the sphere of his accountability. In so doing, he further hollows out the chasm.

[29] *Abraham replied, "They have Moses and the prophets; they should listen to them."*

That Luke includes this statement shows us that for Luke, Jesus stands in profound continuity with his Jewish tradition of prophets. These prophets bear a remarkable unity in the singularity of their judgment on undignified economic spirituality. Their passion is crystallized in Ezekiel's lamentation (28:11–19), speaking God's voice, over the ancient king of Tyre, echoing to our present economy:

> In the abundance of your trade you were filled with violence, and you sinned. . . . Your heart was proud because of your beauty; you corrupted your wisdom for the sake of your splendor . . . in the unrighteousness of your trade, you profaned your sanctuaries. . . . All who know you among the peoples are appalled at you; you have come to a dreadful end and shall be no more forever.

Further, by invoking Moses' name, Luke recalls the reader to verse 19, in which Exodus 25 was intimated. Linking Moses to the prophets here associates Exodus with their teaching. Exodus is the Bible's pri-

mary exhibit of God's concern for the economy, in upending the
Egyptian economy for the liberation of the Israelites.

[30] *He said, "No, father Abraham; but if someone goes to them from the
dead, they will repent."*

The rich man's fear for his family is palpable in his persistence in
disagreement—"no"—with Abraham. Perhaps the rich man shares in
his family's attitude about wealth, as for the first time he speaks of
the need to repent. It is their repentance, however, and not his own,
on which he focuses.

His desperation shows in losing focus on Lazarus and proposing
"someone"—anyone, he almost seems to say. Perhaps Abraham himself can make a personal trip to warn his family?

[31] *He said to him, "If they do not listen to Moses and the prophets, neither will they be convinced even if someone rises from the dead."*

Christians sometimes read these last words too hastily as "convinced [of the gospel, of Christ's reality, of God in Jesus] even if
someone rises from the dead." But recall what is at stake in this story.
The rich man needs convincing of the life-determining spiritual
power of economic spirituality.

With these final words, Luke the gospel writer subtly laments
what he has seen in his own Christian community. Because Luke
writes after Jesus' resurrection, Jesus *has* risen for Luke's community,
and yet Christians are still not convinced of the life-determining spiritual power of economic spirituality—"neither will they be convinced even if someone rises from the dead." Luke has Abraham
sound cynical here, and, perhaps, Luke crafted this passage as an
expression of disappointment, even bitterness.

Here, Luke links the meaning of the resurrection precisely with
economic spirituality. To honor Jesus "rising from the dead" is to avoid
living like the rich man. Salvation happens in and through economic
relationships, before the gate becomes a chasm.

WHAT IS TRULY FAITHFUL LIFE?
THE ULTIMATE STANDARD

Because this story appears only in Luke, some might be tempted to dismiss it as an invention of the author of the Third Gospel. And yet the centrality of economic spirituality is sounded again and again in Christian scripture.

To "inherit eternal life," Jesus says quite directly to the wealthy man, sell all your possessions and give the proceeds to those truly in need (Luke 18:18–25, Matthew 19:16–30, Mark 10:17–31). But let us not get hung up on whether or not one must sell *everything* in order to participate more fully in divine economics. For when Jesus invites himself to dinner at the house of Zacchaeus, the wealthy tax collector (Luke 19:1–10), he takes a different approach. Jesus allows Zacchaeus to come up with a novel plan for discipleship, and we can hear both the pragmatism and the earnestness in Zacchaeus' voice. He does not want to give it all away, but he does say, "Look, half of my possessions, Lord, I will give to the poor; and if I have defrauded anyone of anything, I will pay back four times as much."

Jesus does not merely consider Zacchaeus to be a nice person for this consecration of his resources for the life of others. Jesus pronounces it decisive for Zacchaeus' own existence: "*Today* salvation *has come* to this house, because he too is a son of Abraham." Jesus cannot mean a "son of Abraham" only literally here. It would be redundant for him to affirm that, because Zacchaeus already was so by blood when Jesus arrived. Jesus must mean that Zacchaeus has finally responded in spirit—in spiritual maturity to faith in the God of Abraham. He has truly lived up to the title "son of Abraham." Recall Jesus' story in Luke, in which the rich man's failure of economic spirituality alienated him in the afterlife from Abraham, even though he was ethnically a descendant of Abraham. When Jesus speaks of membership in Abraham's or his own family, he often refers to those whose faith is lived in the struggle of the everyday for decency, dignity, and solidarity. For example, when people praise Jesus' own mother to him, he almost always distances himself from her and redefines who his "family" is. "Whoever *does* the will of God is my brother and sister and mother" (Mark 3:35).

Jesus' approach to discipleship with Zacchaeus is resolutely local and particular—Jesus does not force Zacchaeus into a cookie-cutter response. His program for economic spirituality is different between Zacchaeus (give away half; repair defrauded accounts) and the wealthy man (give away all). Yet while the approach is inflected differently depending on Jesus' pragmatic understanding of the situation, the underlying theme is the same: one's resources are never fully one's own and are to be used for the sake of more life for all, especially those whose lives are most threadbare.

Some of our greatest clarity, however, about a Christian understanding of economic stewardship comes from Matthew 25. This chapter is the New Testament's magnum opus regarding the meaning of a spiritual life. In it, Jesus is pictured as a kingly shepherd separating the sheep from the goats. Those "sheep" who are blessed by God and "inherit the kingdom" go to one side, and those "goats" who are "accursed" go to the other, to "depart . . . into the eternal fire prepared for the devil and his angels."

What is the crucial difference between the sheep and goats? Nothing other than what we have already learned from Lazarus, from the wealthy man, or from Zacchaeus. The sheep are those who fed the hungry, gave drink to the thirsty, welcomed the stranger, clothed the naked, cared for the sick, and visited the prisoner "during their lifetime" (to use the words of Luke 16). In other words, they stewarded their resources for the sake of the flourishing of those in need. (The contrast with the rich man's inordinate concern for his own blood relatives in Luke 16 is striking.) They were economic stewards. The goats, by contrast, have failed to use their freedom and their resources for this stewardship.

This story has two under-recognized dimensions. First, this economic spirituality may be practiced in the most ordinary of ways without ever having to think of God or consciously refer one's activities to God. The "righteous" protest to the shepherd, "*When* was it that we saw you hungry and gave you food, or thirsty and gave you something to drink? When was it that we saw you sick or in prison and visited you?" The shepherd replies that "just as you did it to one of the least of these who are members of my family, you did it to me."

That is to say, whether or not we piously recognize God in the stewardship of our resources, whether or not we think we are being holy or righteous or Godly in our economic discipleship, whether or not we have God consciously on our radar in the way we use our resources for those in need, God honors this relationship manifest in works *regardless*. And this relationship honors God—regardless. We will not always know, says Matthew 25, when we are honoring God—indeed, we *need* not always know this, and perhaps we *cannot* know it—and that is precisely the way in which we do and must live our spirituality. Perhaps knowing it leads to an overfocus on our own piety. Never before did I think that "Just Do It," Nike's long-running brand slogan, would describe the gospel, but it fits here.

But there is a second unusual dimension. This passage in its breathtaking radicality goes beyond Christians to imply that *all* people's lives will be so judged by God in this way. When Matthew writes that "all the nations" (v.32) will be assembled before the king, he is using a Hebraic term to refer to all those who may not know God. "The nations," in fact, are often the "gentiles" in the Hebrew Bible. In other words, all people may meaningfully practice this stewardship in the most ordinary of ways without ever having to think of God or consciously refer their activities to God; and God will endorse and bless their work.

Matthew 25 suggests that economic spirituality is part of the fundamental orientation for or against God that we take in our living. The spiritual challenge of these passages to us in a branded economy is nothing more nor less than an enlargement of what salvation is, what love of God means. This spirituality is so central to the meaning of faith that in the final analysis, we can question our faith, leave our religious institutions, and doubt God's existence, and still, if we give ourselves in maturity to the responsibilities of our economic relationships, we can do what we may and ask God to bless the difference.

One second-century record of Christian teaching summarized well Jesus' economic spirituality by proclaiming, "The Father wants his own gifts to be universally shared."[1]

ON NOT CONTROLLING
OTHERS ECONOMICALLY

As God's economist, Jesus reveals a way of being in the world both economic and spiritual.

Economically, he signals that redistribution of resources in the direction of those in need of them should be a normal and even central concern for a person growing in spiritual maturity. Why? Precisely for theological reasons: our lack of final ownership of our resources is rooted in our lack of ownership of the God who ultimately creates all. God is not at our disposal. As the trusted mystery, God is the uncontrollable. As the gracious Creator on whom our goods depend, our goods participate in God's uncontrollability. As in the encounter with that power on which we all depend, we can only render ourselves faithful stewards of our gifts.

CHAPTER 3

TODAY'S SPIRITUAL DISCIPLINE:

THE BRAND ECONOMY

Given the prominent scriptural focus on right economic relationships, why is this focus so often undervalued in contemporary Christian life?

Churches have innovated many escape hatches to avoid the Scriptures' economic spirituality, and one always has to be wary of how these escape hatches are defined and controlled by the church (just as one must critically examine, I should add, any theologian's claims). These escape hatches proffer a way to avoid our economic responsibilities, and they go by many names disguised as keys to Christian life: overfocusing on individual sexual morality, issuing woes about the secular culture, or reducing Christian faith to a verbal act of "confessing Jesus," which is probably the most common Christian heresy in America. Even liberal church leaders can liquidate economic spirituality by guilt-tripping their congregations, which is usually a form of clerical paternalism.

We can also, however, look to our branding culture to understand why Christians neglect the scriptural economic focus. Branding is a sort of religious system, a spiritual discipline, that can provide as persuasive a worldview as the scriptures or any traditional religion.

When these escape hatches—attacks on sex, "secularism," "consumerism," or promotions of "the name of Jesus"—are substituted for the gateway of economic spirituality, then we are dealing with a kind of cheap grace, submitting ourselves too uncritically to the moral codes of religious institutions rather than asking anew what right economic relationships require today.

THE BIG TURN-OFF: MORALIZING

For a long time, I resisted looking at the seamy underside of our brand economy. I did so not because I endorsed its abuses; underpaid and overworked women toiling over sewing machines had yet to interrupt my still-too-suburban imagination. I resisted looking critically at branding partly as a reaction to mostly liberal Christians who moralize about it. I was overreacting against what I thought was *their* predisposition to overreact.

These Christians demonize young people and all who unwittingly participate in what they simplistically dismiss as "consumer culture." They declaim that once-quality products are now manufactured cheaply, that advertising manipulates impressionable young minds irremediably into malleable and obedient consumers, and that even life itself has been commodified. Capitalism, they say, erects a carnival of Pavlovian delights disguised as the brand economy, and those who do not opt out have sold out.

I agree with theologian Robert Schreiter that "blanket demonization[s] of capitalism" are unhelpful.[1] Demonizing or moralizing about our brand economy is too simplistic an approach when dealing with human beings who struggle secretly as well as publicly to make do in this economy, who have the power to resist its lures, and who often innovate nonspectacular ways to subvert its control over their everyday lives.

Such moralizing, most notoriously by academics or ministers, exhales a humid mixture of condescension, guilt, and envy. It condescends to the supposedly less mature. I should know; I adopted the strategies of my imagined liberal oppressors soon after I read

Naomi Klein. At several conferences, I delivered sober jeremiads about the economic passivity of my generation and our implication in the exploitation of poor workers overseas. The nadir of my thundering happened after I had just spoken to several thousand Christians at an evangelical conference in Hawaii. On my way out of the arena afterward, a woman rushed up to me and grasped my hand and arm, gushing "Thank you! Thank you for that spiritual spanking you gave me!"

In that moment, I realized that being shamed into guilt was one way for Christians to avoid taking responsibility. There can actually be a spiritual *frisson* in scolding and being scolded, being reduced to a feeling of utter dependence on God—but on a God present most intensively in self-flagellation. Although I had many laughs about it later, I never wanted to give another talk that someone would experience as a "spiritual spanking."

Moralizing was a way of redirecting my own guilt over my inability to change my economic practices. It was also a way of conveying my resentment that the costs of my discipleship—my sacrifices for my faith—were not being recognized by others. My moralizing was an expression of my envy that other people were not as troubled by their habits of consumption as I was becoming. The spanker is often also the spankee.

The theologian Karl Rahner spotted the petty pedantry that so often seems to attend Christian life. He argued that "the church should be one which defends morality boldly and unambiguously, without moralizing." For Rahner, moralizers

> expound norms of behavior peevishly and pedantically, full of moral indignation at a world without morals, without really tracing them back to that innermost experience of human nature . . . the living Spirit, the message of freedom from merely external law, the message of love which is no longer subject to any law when it prevails.[2]

In other words, moralizing appeals only to people's guilt by emphasizing their failure to live up to certain external standards. Moralizing attempts to embarrass people into action by piously berating them or their habits. It replaces thinking; it substitutes the incitement of guilt for a real economic analysis.

But morality can be defended without moralizing. Rahner reminds us that defending morality requires referring people to their freedom, to our ability to be guided by the Spirit. Defending morality means appealing to our ability to act otherwise than we currently do, to make something in our lives—if not all things—genuinely new.

One challenge for thinking people of faith, then, is to try to understand why the branding economy is as successful as it is, without falling into a moralizing interpretation—that is, without making people think that they are (paradoxically) guilty robots. I find that avoiding moralizing is tremendously difficult, and I am sure my own interpretation falls short on certain points. Indeed, I have come very close to moralizing about moralizing in the paragraphs above.

Rahner is a fine example of a person of faith who tried to avoid moralizing, on the one hand, and a failure to make genuine faith judgments, on the other. The same Rahner who warned against moralizing also said that there are

> hidden but deeply rooted falsifications of genuine Christianity that have not reached the level of consciousness, but that are much worse and more important than certain officially designated heresies. . . . It could well be that, for example, a certain large-city or small-town bourgeois mentality of conservative bent is fundamentally a much greater heresy, even though it is so seldom singled out as such, than if someone were to say that there are no angels, or that one could not imagine what original sin could be.[3]

Inspired by his challenge to think carefully about moral issues without lapsing into moralizing, I want to risk thinking through why our brand economy has such power to organize our lives, to do identity work for us, to dissuade Christians from the scripture's sense of economic spirituality—so as to make judicious moral judgments about it all.

BRANDING NATURE

One summer, I was on retreat at St. John's University in Collegeville, Minnesota. A Benedictine monastery there rests atop a hill overlooking hundreds of forested acres, as well as an immense rippling gray-blue lake, a Midwestern Sea of Galilee. One bright and breezy day, after lunch, I walked behind the abbey church to take in the lake's pacific immensity, a million-gallon basin of holy water surrounded by the Minnesotan "Black Forest" so prized by the monastery's German founders.

Stepping sideways down the grassy slope, gloriously alone, I approached the water's edge with a reverence that surprised me, alive on all sides to the high blueness of the sky radiating somehow upward through grass, tree, lake, and dirt path.

Giving myself to this nature that evolves so much more patiently than my soul's hurried urban meter, I was aware of a new element in my perceptual field. To my lower left was a circular blue, white, and red blur. There was nothing new on the lake or in the forest itself; this object was a mental projection, thrown by my mind onto the scene. With surprised disappointment, I soon recognized the amorphous blur as a soft drink logo.

A few hours earlier, I had eaten lunch in a student dining room. Across the top of one of the soft drink machines was a pleasant, 12-inch by 3-foot photo of the very lakescape in which I was at that moment reveling—the sun also high in the sky, the armor of green forest protecting the watery bowl. But this picture featured a soft drink logo in the corner, affixing a cola identity to this refuge from all things branded. Seeing the ad struck me as a petty obscenity, evidence that the soda's advertisers were aware of the lake's spiritual power and, yet, oblivious to the holiness of areas sacrosanct from branding. I guessed that because the soft drink company could not erect a billboard on the water's edge, they reproduced the lake scene and branded the reproduction.

In the dining area, few students seemed to notice the ad. Perhaps they ignore it, "jamming" its presence by buying other sodas or other such strategies. Maybe, overwhelmed by logos, they develop an indifference to such symbols. Or, perhaps for them, it eventually becomes part of their perceptual horizon, rarely conscious, but for just that reason all the more influential.

On the bank, what was most evident was the thing not actually there. While I was impressed by the soft drink's ability to use a spiritual strategy, identifying its product with a scene that addressed my soul, I wondered what I would have to do to unlearn the logo.

THE BRAND ECONOMY
AS A SPIRITUAL DISCIPLINE

The branding economy works through such schooling of imagination. But to recognize as much is to name only one way that this economy works to shape us. It works in part because of its unique dynamic: branding also offers a consistent, coherent identity, in which you are told about your true self; it offers membership in a community; it issues an invitation to unconditional trust; it offers the promise of conversion and new life. Thus, there is a way of life, an identity, that can be had by participating in the logo-centric economy. These are, after all, worthwhile ends and even deep human needs.

But the formation of imagination, a true self, community, trust, and new life are not only ways by which the economy offers a way of life. This dynamic is also found in many classic spiritual disciplines. And so I propose that by looking at the way a classic spiritual discipline works through these strategies, we can better understand the branding economy. In other words, the brand economy can be seen as a Western spiritual discipline. (And, though I will not pursue it here, spiritual disciplines may be seen as brand economies.) The economy, as a spiritual discipline, is not consciously "spiritual" or "religious," but it operates with a dynamic similar to classic spiritual disciplines—anonymously, if you will. This is no mere academic fantasy. "Brand managers" in the business world often think in such terms. "Corporate branding," according to one manager, "is really about worldwide beliefs management."[4] The management of beliefs is the work of a spiritual discipline.

When I compare our brand economy to classic spiritual disciplines, I am thinking of rules of prayer and life such as the *Spiritual Exercises* of St. Ignatius. Most people do not consider these spiritual disciplines on the whole to be moralizing or dangerously controlling. On the contrary, due to the influence of authors like Kathleen Norris, Paul Mariani, and Thomas Merton, spiritual disciplines are today in the flower of widespread rebirth. This is in part because all authentic spiritual disciplines respond to basic human spiritual needs. Thus, if we use classic spiritual disciplines as a counterpart for the brand economy, we have some hope that we will avoid a moralizing interpretation of the economy.

ST. IGNATIUS' *EXERCISES*

Ignatius of Loyola (1491–1556) was a mercurial and dramatic Spanish nobleman. Like St. Augustine, he lived a passionate young adulthood, bent on a life of status in the Spanish court, enlivened by serial amorous conquests, and edified by chivalrous novels, which in their own way were the romance fiction of his day. After being injured on the battlefield during a foolhardy stand against the French, Ignatius befriended God while lying in bed for months nursing a leg shattered by cannonfire. While recuperating, he began to read books about the lives of Jesus and the saints, and decided to commit his life fully to God. Also like Augustine, his conversion did not mean that his past was overcome. His spiritual contemplation contended with daydreams about wooing a noble woman, and his former visions of a knightly career later transmogrified into the service of Christ the King and the defense of the honor of that noble Lady, the Virgin Mary. This, to be sure, did not turn him into a dour man. In warm tribute, one of his friends wrote that "those who were in his room were continually laughing."[5]

In service of this new allegiance to Christ—one marked by a deep emotional identification with the saints, Mary, and Jesus—Ignatius eventually founded the Society of Jesus, known as the Jesuits, for the purpose of educating and saving souls. His two decades of traveling, reading spiritual books and philosophy, and noticing the movements of his own interior life, resulted in a famous handbook called *The Spiritual Exercises*, published in 1548. It is something like a "teacher's guide" for retreat directors. People today, however, frequently use the *Exercises* for personal and communal prayer without going on formal retreats.

The purposes of those retreats, and therefore of the *Exercises*, were to encourage union with God, and to facilitate the retreatant making a decision about their way of life that would glorify God. In practice, Ignatius often seemed to use the *Exercises* as a tool to sift out potential candidates for his emerging society, though sometimes he led people through the *Exercises* and they made dramatic changes in their lives—such as giving up possessions—without necessarily joining his motley crew of itinerant preachers.

The *Exercises* are divided into four weeks of "exercises"—or work-outs, if you will—which are an assortment of practices of prayer, guided visualization, meditation, attention to feelings, imagined conversations, and self-examinations. By working through them, one advances along a journey of mindfulness of one's own sin, desire for Christ-like virtues, and closer union with God through an intimate sharing in Christ's sufferings and joys. Ignatius includes a wealth of sidebars on working through spiritually sticky situations, such as rules for discerning good from evil spirits influencing you, rules for thinking and feeling with the Church, rules for those who struggle with debilitating guilt about sin, and methods for examination of conscience. The *Exercises* is one of the classic spiritual handbooks of Western Christianity.

All Jesuits resource the *Exercises* for regular retreats; it is the roadmap for their spiritual formation. But many others use it, too. Indeed, there has been a remarkable passion among lay Christians of all traditions, and other curious seekers, to learn about the *Spiritual Exercises*. Whatever the reasons for this recent cloudburst of curiosity about spiritual discipline, churches around the United States are now increasingly making use of Ignatius' methods for becoming more open to spiritual maturity, for fostering, as he put it, "ease in finding God."[6]

IMAGINATION AS A HUMAN POWER

The soda advertisement at St. John's had trained my imagination to associate a logo with the lake. Such is just a taste of the power of imagination to structure our everyday experience, even our spiritual lives. Each of us, for example, relies on our own image—that is imaginative rendering—of God. Our images of God are drawn from our experience of our parents, our formal and informal religious education, and a host of other significant life experiences we have had.

Imagination is a power that all humans have to put together our observations and experiences in a particular way, to find patterns of meaning in the observations, insights, feelings, and experiences of everyday life. Far from being the preserve of Tolkienesque fantasy, we each live everyday life utterly dependent on our imaginations. Who do you imagine yourself to be now, and who do you imagine yourself becoming? As philosopher Paul Ricoeur observed, "in imagining possibilities, human beings act as the prophets of their own existence."[7]

Almost all significant interactions with our world are influenced by our imaginations. What do we make of our life's work? How do we picture the meaning of our families? Even, who is Jesus (Buddha? Abraham?)? We are all confronted with immense emotional, physical, intellectual, psychological data about ourselves, our families, our work—even our God. As if gathering stars or clouds together into meaningful shapes, our imaginations constellate our life perceptions into coherent patterns (I am *this* sort of person; my family is *this* way, my work means *this*).

To use a simple example, I am always surprised by the imaginative capacities of friends when they have helped me move from apartment to apartment (15 times in the last 15 years). A few friends have a consummate ability to look at disorderly piles of furniture, boxes, and loose knickknacks and imagine how it all will fit with extreme efficiency into whatever truck, van, or car I have procured. They can easily imagine the pieces arranged, secure, and orderly. I once thought that my inability to do what they do indicated that my imagination was somehow malformed, that I simply needed to try harder. Maybe,

I thought, my imagination was unripe spatially, and I could be trained to learn to organize space "better."

I have learned over the years that it is not that I have a defective imagination regarding moving my stuff. I have had to admit to myself that I am drawn to imagine my stuff as needing to exist in some kind of creative disarray. That is, in part, what I imagine makes it *my* stuff. So I have to work even more diligently if I want to be an asset during moving time to my friends who imagine more orderly arrangements of household stuff. This it not to say that my imagination cannot be trained anymore, but that the effect of thirty years of imagining disorder as divine is hard to undo in one stressful moving day. (One significant informer of my imagination in this regard was a sign in the basement of a friend's house in which we used to play Dungeons and Dragons: "Creative minds are rarely tidy.")

IMAGINATION IN IGNATIUS

Ignatius recognized the power of imagination over our spiritual lives by giving it lots of attention in the *Exercises*. He constantly encourages the "exercitant"—the one undergoing the exercises—to be mindful of their imaginative capacities as they prepare to pray.

Two ways of aiding the imagination stand out. First, Ignatius exhorts the exercitant to imagine him- or herself in a setting conducive to a particular meditation. These imaginings are called compositions or representations. Ignatius writes that we can imagine visible settings, such as being present with Jesus in the temple, perhaps to draw spiritual fruit from this story. Or we can imagine "abstract and invisible" settings, such as imagining our soul as "imprisoned" in the body, and feeling our embodied souls as exiled in a valley surrounded by dangerous animals, perhaps to contemplate the peril our soul has been in due to sin.[8]

Sometimes the compositions challenge the exercitant into a commonplace setting from another age. To foster deeper union with God through sympathy with Christ's sufferings at the last supper, Ignatius asks the retreatant to "see in imagination the road from Bethany to Jerusalem, whether it is broad, or narrow, or level, and so on. In similar manner, imagine the room of the supper, whether it is large, or small, or arranged in one way or another."[9]

At other times, the compositions are dramatic. During the second week, Ignatius has the exercitant imagine two "standards" or opposing chieftains, Christ and Lucifer. On an expansive plain near Jerusalem stands the community under Christ, and arrayed near Babylon stands the people of Lucifer. Christ and Lucifer colorfully direct their charges into the world, the former by sending out diverse disciples to "aid all persons," and the latter by choreographing "uncountable devils," who ensnare people in riches, honor, and pride, directed by Lucifer "on a throne of fire and smoke, in aspect horrible and terrifying."[10] One of the points of this imaginative exercise is meditation on the source of the virtues or vices in one's life, and therefore the necessity of choosing an ethical source well. (A much more banal example from my childhood would be the choosing of teams in kickball during recess; one has finally to play on one side or the other, helping the team and captain to victory. There is no third option, unless of course you don't want to play kickball in the first place. The power of Ignatius' imaginative suggestion is that almost everyone considers themselves to have some virtues and/or vices.)

Another way Ignatius uses imagination is through conversations with biblical figures. These are called colloquies and are frequently used in the *Exercises*. The exercitant imagines that they are talking directly with a scriptural persona, sometimes in the biblical scene itself, and sometimes detached from it, but always in a very personal and intimate way. Ignatius writes that a colloquy happens "in the way one friend speaks to another, or a servant to one in authority—now begging a favor, now accusing oneself of some misdeed, now telling one's concerns and asking counsel about them."[11]

After contemplating the mystery of God's redemption of humanity through the incarnation of Jesus, Ignatius recommends that the exercitant consider speaking directly to God the Trinity, or to Christ, or Mary. This is no mere academic discourse or perfunctory recitation. "I will beg favors," Ignatius boldly states, "according to what I feel in my heart, that I may better follow and imitate our Lord."[12]

Perhaps the most famous colloquy happens during the first week of exercises, when the exercitant is to imagine Jesus hanging on the cross in front of them, and they are free to talk with him. This colloquy has always had a gruesome power for me, because it suggests addressing Jesus as he is dying. That intense gift and burden: a coherent and intimate conversation in the final stages of death. Ignatius suggests that you ask Jesus about the mystery of his life and suffering on earth. Further, that you ask yourself the following questions: "What have I done for Christ? What am I doing for Christ? What ought I to do for Christ?" And finally, Ignatius exhorts you to have the courage of the full intimacy of this moment, to involve yourself in the losing of this dying man . . . "gazing on him in so pitiful a state as he hangs on the cross, speak out whatever comes to your mind."[13]

When meditating on the Last Supper during the third week of exercises, Ignatius tells the exercitant to "see the persons at the Supper," to "listen to what they are saying," and to "see what they are doing," in order to benefit spiritually from all these imaginings. The New Testament gives very little detail about what the persons looked like, and the dialogue and actions are sparsely recounted. In giving so much attention to imagination, Ignatius wants you to insert yourself into the scenes of scripture, utterly personalizing them, by filling in the missing dialogue, actions, thoughts, and feelings. Rehearsing scripture in this way is a profoundly imaginative act.

Eventually, in the Ignatian discipline, your imagination should be so formed that you are more able to perceive or experience God in all things. But one does not get there quickly. The four weeks of exercises are only the beginning of the training of the imagination, the fruits of which appear not necessarily during the official retreat time itself, but in the daily life to which one returns afterward. Thus, continual practice of these imaginative exercises is a natural part of an Ignatian discipline. To reorient persons spiritually, Ignatius knew, one had to reshape them imaginatively.

I have dwelled at some length on imagination, because formation of imagination is, in my view, the most important "strategy" of the branding economy. On this strategy all of its other successes depends.

Without being able to influence our imaginations, the economy cannot shape our perceptions of our true self, our relation to a community, our investments of trust, and our hope for a new life. I am not suggesting that the economy (or the Ignatian discipline) controls imagination, only that the imagination is inclined or encouraged by these disciplines in specific directions.

In short, without the power of the economy to shape our imaginations, the economy would fail as an anonymous spiritual discipline—and the branding economy itself would buckle, collapse, and disintegrate. I am not calling for anything so apocalyptic: only a meager first step, which is that we become more aware of and responsible for the ways in which brands influence our imaginations and encourage a discipline in us.

IMAGINATION IN THE BRANDING ECONOMY

The branding economy shapes our imaginations with a potential power so formative of identity that it can only be called spiritual (this is not to say that it is a healthy or unhealthy spirituality at this point—to do so would too quickly shift us back to moralizing about the economy). In chapter 1, I discussed my own and my students' abilities to describe the identity work for which we use different brands, the clarity of brand meanings, and how our imaginations about identity change as we identify with certain brands.

To develop an example I used in chapter 1, we can see this influence on imagination at work in the phenomenon of one popular cable television show. Earlier, I discussed how certain brands of hair care products catered to women who identified with a particular character on the show. After the discussion of imagination above, we can now see more clearly that part of what is happening in such an economic event is that some women are being encouraged to imagine themselves as one of the show's characters, or at least as capable of taking on some of their qualities. The mediator for this imagination is the brand, which will help young adult women fashion a hairstyle that promises access to the personalities valorized in the show.

In addition to looking at the ability of specific brands to influence imagination, some researchers have taken a broader view, examining ways that Americans share a common consumer imagination oriented to typical consumer fantasies. According to the sociological research of Susan Fournier and Michael Guiry, consumer fantasies can be categorized with some reliability. Such fantasies include widespread desires for new and better homes, new cars, and luxury items such as jewelry and designer clothes. (Fournier and Guiry also found a broadening of the meaning of materialism in consumer fantasies, to include "enhancement of self, family, and society" through consumer goods, and consumer fantasies themselves as pleasurable goods of consumer society.)[14] Imagining a more fulfilled self and community included desires for an indentifiable set of products.

In his research on consumer fantasies, John Caughey found that

> Despite some systematic variation in social roles and subcultural affiliations, middle-class Americans seem to share a very similar fantasy life. The recurrent fantasies of my informants fall into only seven major classes: career success, alternate career success, natural world escape, material wealth, successful violence, sex-romance, and blissful married life, [and] any given fantasy often includes. . . several of the other topics.[15]

In one typical example, Caughey's research revealed that "[f]antasy descriptions of ideal houses often sound like commercials, and many can be traced directly to particular media productions."[16]

Our imaginations about a successful self and community have come to be mediated by the brand economy. The brand represents a lifestyle or an attitude that we dream can become our own. In the words of economist Robert H. Nelson, "stepping into 'daydreams' motivates the modern consumer, who looks to the realization of such fantasies virtually as his or her own artistic project."[17] In the words of social scientist Colin Campbell, our economy is driven by a "longing to experience in reality those pleasures created and enjoyed in imagination."[18]

INITIATION INTO TRUE SELF

In spiritual disciplines, one's imagination is often influenced for the sake of a different understanding of oneself. We can, if we practice such disciplines, change our very sense of our identity, reorient how we understand our true selves. In other words, disciplines can influence the way you relate to yourself by forming your imagination about yourself. Every discipline attempts to persuade you of the truth about yourself.

For Ignatius, your true self is as whole person, body-and-soul. He imagines that each person has a role to play in God's plan for the redemption of the world, and the glorification of creatures—an eternal destiny of happiness, in unending intimacy with God, to which all humans are called. Ignatius summarizes this conviction in something like a "mission statement" for the human race:

> Human beings are created to praise, reverence and serve God our Lord, and by means of this to save their souls. The other things on the face of the earth are created for the human beings, to help them in working toward the end for which they are created. From this it follows that I should use these things to the extent that they help me toward my end, and rid myself of them to the extent that they hinder me . . . I ought to desire and elect only the thing which is more conducive to the end for which I am created. (#23)

In other words, this discipline encourages us to see ourselves as part of God's salvific plan for creation, as having our own unique role, which we are fully able to "desire and elect" (or choose).

In the branding economy, the true self is a many faceted economic being: a consumer of a favored brand; a producer of meaning, status, or identity through your interaction with brands; an advertiser for corporations when you willingly billboard yourself by displaying logos on your body, in your house, through your speech. What is most important about your relation to yourself, then, is the way that relation passes through the screen of the brand. You cannot inhabit your full self without passing through brands, just as you cannot fully inhabit a house without passing through doorways. Others have come to similar insights: "That we are what we have is perhaps the most basic and powerful fact of consumer behavior."[19]

This is evident in the proliferation of television shows and movies that emphasize "makeovers" with branded products that give women or men a more attractive sheen. One does not have to be against beauty or sexiness to question the deep association with these branded hair and makeup products with access to true self-expression. As Alissa Quart suggests, "makeover movies" like two very popular teen films of the last decade "claim that the girls being powdered and primped and branded are becoming their 'true' selves."[20]

MEMBERSHIP IN COMMUNITY

Although the *Spiritual Exercises* can be read straight through like a book, doing so in private was the furthest thing from Ignatius' intention. To the contrary, one purpose of experiencing this discipline is to initiate the exercitant into the community of the church. This community is represented by the spiritual director who walks through the retreat with the exercitant. Community is so important for Ignatius that he gives guidelines for integrating more fully into it, called "Rules for Thinking, Judging, and Feeling with the Church." These rules emphasize obedience to and defense of the institutional church, as well as pious service. (Ignatius was so intent on the maintenance of community that he included the famous claim, "What I see as white, I will believe to be black if the hierarchical Church thus determines it.")[21]

Community is also made available to those of us who participate in the branding economy. By identifying with a brand of video game, I can join an online community of players from around the world who gather late into the night to maim, torch, insult, gossip, chat, and compete against each other, and for whom the "virtual" gamescape often becomes a more real venue for soul-baring and confession than any "real" church setting.

By wearing certain brands of clothing, we purchase our way into music communities. Music journalist Chuck Klosterman recounts how the bassist for one rap-rock band was startled by fans' willingness to adorn themselves in the same brand of sneakers as the band. "I remember the first time we toured as headliners, and I looked out the window of the bus. Every kid was wearing" this brand of sneakers. "It was an entire crowd of kids who dressed the way we do. We called [the sneaker company] and told them they owed us money."[22]

By manifesting certain sportswear logos, we become participants in communities of athletes or athlete-sympathizers. Or perhaps we wrest the logos away from their original context and use them for other forms of community, as when gangs co-opt sporting and fashion logos to construct their own symbols for sociality. Moreover, many bands today have become their own brand, and owning CDs or other band-related products initiates one into a community of fans, fraternizing at concerts, at the mall, or online. Even coffee brands become symbols for community. Writing of his remarkably successful coffee shop chain, one entrepreneur emphasized "the romance of the coffee experience, the feeling of warmth and community people get" in these shops.[23] And on one cable television show's website, by clicking on "community," you can participate in chat rooms that discuss the characters and their fashions. Much of the discussion in the fashion chat room focuses on the brands the characters are wearing and where they might be purchased, especially on the cheap.

INVITATION TO TRUST

God, according to Ignatius, is one who satisfies authentic desires. Thus, God—and ultimately only God—can be absolutely and unconditionally trusted. Throughout the *Exercises*, Ignatius encourages the retreatant to "ask God our Lord for what I want and desire," trusting that we are capable of truly desiring things lead us to our proper vocation of praise, reverence, and service of God.

Similarly, one of the most apparent strategies of the logo-heavy economy is the way in which it encourages us to trust in the logo. Our relative trust in logos is overwhelmingly evident in Americans' refusal to ask critical questions about where our branded products come from, who produced them, and how they were produced. We allow the logo to fill up our visualscape, as if there were room to see nothing else about the product except its immediate reality in front of us, and its corresponding gesture to a lifestyle.

Trust is invested in logos, which have become symbols that have religious power to induce dependence, a feeling with religious significance. For the nineteenth-century Protestant theologian Friedrich Schleiermacher, the feeling of absolute dependence was the same as being in relation with God.[24] Corporations see brands as "expressions of the soul" of the firm, beneficently establishing "covenant" with consumers, and extending a "brand promise."[25] Consumers are invited to trust this promise and covenant, the soul of the firm. They are successful when, in the words of youth researcher Alissa Quart, teenagers "feel that consumer goods are their friends—and that the companies selling products to them are trusted allies."[26]

Indeed, whereas religious institutions on the whole have been increasingly drained of trustworthiness in the last several decades, our economy has been so invested with it that in the words of theologian Harvey Cox, we treat not just brands but the "market as God"— omnipotent, omniscient, and omnipresent, inscrutable in its ways, and capable of doing nothing truly harmful to us. We need only render our full trust in this market-as-God and all will be well. The symbols of this God—our logos—are evident in our secular cathedrals. Naomi Klein, for instance, argues that one footwear store in New York City is functionally a "temple" to the shoe's omnipresent logo.[27]

And in one of those seemingly irrelevant details that end up revealing the code of the whole system, one diamond company reported that it would imprint its logo in extraordinarily small lettering on stones greater than one carat. "The logo will be visible," it was reported, "only under 200-times magnification."[28] The word "magnification" is a theological term indicating high praise, immense laud, intensive and expansive gratitude, exultation. That this logo is visible only when magnified 200 times symbolizes the demand logos are placing on us for adoration, laud, high favor. As if the logo had to appear so small on one product, somewhere, in order to illustrate in a definitive way the magnification of the logo that already exists everywhere in our society. As if this diamond and its tiny symbol are the incarnation and crystallization of the postmodern economy, the logos of the logo.

PROMISE OF NEW LIFE

Finally, spiritual disciplines work a new life in you. We become different people than we were before giving ourselves to the discipline. Our sense of what is possible for ourselves changes. In the *Exercises*, this new way of being is known in part through making a spiritually sound choice about what to do with your life. Although Ignatius does have a bias that the vowed celibate life is holier than the married life, he otherwise does not attempt to control the specific outcomes of decisions people make about their lives through the use of the *Exercises*. He only gives guidelines for being prayerfully in a spiritual posture where the horizon of a new life can appear to us. He recommends, most especially, cultivating "indifference" to important choices about a way of life with which we are faced. By indifference, he means allowing oneself not to be overly invested in a decision about a way of life turning out one way or the other, to neither overly desire nor disown a life option for ourselves when confronted with what to do. Keeping in mind our proper end (praising of God and salvation of soul), and attending to discerning how God's Spirit is influencing us, will eventually lead us to a decision we can trust. God's dynamism within us is toward new life, through our own good decision making.[29]

The promise of new identity through the brand is also evident. Quart describes how teenagers today are encouraged to take up brand personalities by becoming "[fancy brand deleted] girls or [well-known mall brand] chicks or [another mall brand] boys." What is required is that they purchase "a whole set of clothes from one manufacturer."[30]

There are also books that are a kind of traveling companion to television shows, allowing young adults to see exactly which brands their favorite stars are wearing.

There is no shortage of paths to a new life. One book about a show features photographs of specific brands of sweaters, scarves, shoes,

dresses, "playsuits," pantsuits, bags, coats, gloves, jeans, hats, tops, jewelry, brooches, watches, skirts, boots, cardigans, belts, and purses. The
brands of these clothing items become matched with the personalities of the show's stars. The brands suggest particular personalities
that can be accessorized, in a manner of speaking, by the viewer. By
watching only one episode, or through browsing the show's website,
one quickly learns that one character is (in the words of the show's
fashion designer) an "optimistic, ever-hopeful American girl . . .
preppy and clean cut." Another character would never go out
without makeup, is "always head-to-toe done, nothing delicate or
petite, an out-there gal . . . colorful, outspoken, low-cut . . . glam-
orous." Her personality and clothing "pops in size and color." A third is
"straightforward," alternately "ethnic" and "hippie" in self-
presentation, "quiet and understated." Finally, the main star herself
underwent an evolution from being "thrift-shoppy, downtownish" to
a "designer, smart-girl" look. All of these are personality options corre-
lated to different branded products on the show, and in all the media
that attend the show.

All of these aspects of the discipline of the brand economy are
captured well in an industry phrase reported in a popular U.S. newspaper. In describing contemporary race car drivers who act as human
billboards for specific companies, reporter Chris Jenkins relates that
today, "you're not just a race car driver with a Fortune 500 company's
logo on your fire suit, you're a 'steward of the brand.'"[31] The religious
language is striking: to steward a tradition or a good is to maintain its
vitality and power for the next generation, to hand on to one's juniors
the gift you were given by your seniors. The brand economy would
happily see younger generations as "stewards of the brand," religiously
protecting and maintaining brand identities for their peers, siblings,
and hopefully some day, their children.

RESISTING MORALIZING

My discussion of the brand economy as a sort of spiritual discipline is
biased toward highlighting its dangers and superficialities. While I per-

sonally am willing to invest more of my self in the Ignatian discipline than in the economic discipline, I am aware of my own temptation to overdraw a simplistic separation between a "true" or freeing spiritual discipline and a "false" or manipulative one. To lapse into such a cheap dualism would be to return to the predictable and trite strategies of moralizing. It would, however, take an entirely separate book to look at the ways in which Ignatius' use of imagination, selfhood, community, trust, and conversion are themselves like a brand economy.

But we *must* hold out this possibility—that every religious system that criticizes the economy is *itself* a dangerous economy—if we are to remain intellectually honest. Wherever you try to play an absolutely "true" way of life against an absolutely "false" one, you always must remain open to slippage back and forth: that you will discover more of the "true" and "false" within each other than you thought, and that your attempt to separate the "true" way of life finally from the "false" is due as much to your own anxiety about ambiguity as about any objective difference between, say, Ignatius' discipline and the branding economy.

For the last many years, I have been interested in the spiritual meaning of fashion. Seeing the brand economy as an anonymous spiritual discipline has helped me personally to resist moralizing to myself about the economy, because it has helped me understand the way in which my consumption is—for better and worse—a part of an everyday discipline in my life. What I wear is part of who I am becoming spiritually. On the one hand, this provides comfort because it shows me that what I buy is not outside of my overall spiritual life. On the other hand, it provides great discomfort because I am even more responsible now for making good decisions about what I buy. Brands do not control us, but they do strongly influence us. It is important to keep in mind that young adults—and all consumers—are not robots. We all act with a certain degree of freedom and freely derive some pleasure from our consumption. But that freedom always takes place within a specific context or situation—and the brand economy is the place where a tug-of-war over spiritual discipline happens daily for many young adults.

We can and do use brands as part of a secular spiritual discipline. Becoming more mature spiritually about how we use our consuming, our brands—and which brands we use, and why—is not something *separate* from most young adult lives. Instead, such spiritual responsibility, such economic spirituality, is already implied by the way that young adults relate to the economy.

CHAPTER 4

BODIES AND BRANDING

In the fall of 1999, I called corporate headquarters of one well-known coffee corporation to find out how my favorite coffee was produced, coffee on which I was spending well over $1,000 a year. I found out that they did not deal directly with the Latin American farmers who harvested coffee beans for them. Instead, they employed middle men who handled all dealings with these impoverished farmers. With this business strategy, the coffee corporation kept itself from being held directly responsible for the unhealthy and pitiful living and working conditions of the workers on whom the very quality of their product depended.

In the spring of 2000, I called my way up the food chain of a major sneaker company to find out where my favorite shoes were made, shoes I had been wearing for over a decade, and whose logo I had been proudly displaying on my feet, a walking billboard for a cool brand. I discovered that the company had shut down their American production plant and had moved to China, where the workers would not make a living wage, and where the company did not allow independent inspections of working conditions. Nor would the company release information about overtime pay, average hours per week worked, or benefits for their contracted Chinese factory workers.

In the summer of 2001, having just purchased two pair of trendy and somewhat expensive shoes in downtown Boston, I emailed the corporate headquarters of the company to find out how these unusual shoes were produced. After disclosing that all shoe production occurs in Poland, the spokesman refused to release any information about workers' wages, benefits, working conditions, plant location, or hours—or even the location of the factory.

THE UNDERSIDE OF OUR BRANDS

In the last decade, the veil has been dramatically lifted on the conditions in which many of our branded products are made. Many people have heard or read about large factories, or "sweatshops," where some famous brands assemble products for pennies that get sold in the United States at hundreds or thousands of percentage points' markup. But sometimes we assume that the cases we hear about in the news are only the most appalling cases, that everything else must be basically okay or else those companies would turn up in the news, as well. But as anyone who has tried to find out where their branded goods come from can tell you, the reason for lack of reporting about these issues in the press is not from lack of real news, but from lack of access to information about companies' actual practices. Many companies go to extraordinary length to mislead the public about the production of their goods, or to keep consumers (and the press) in the dark about the who, what, when, where, how, and why of brand production. And because the public has only a limited stomach for such topics, the press is not encouraged to pursue the problem in its depth.

Still, experiences like those of Bangladeshi women are too common to be ignored. In 2002, several women from one Bangladeshi factory, garment workers, gave testimony in the United States about their experiences. One woman named Lisa Rahman, who sewed products for a licensee to a major American corporation, told of conditions that many Americans think of as passé as the world of Dickens. In this factory that employed young women, talking was forbidden, work days stretched to 14 hours, 7 days a week. Slapping and verbal abuse were common. Though she needed 37 cents an hour to "live with a little dignity," she was paid only 14 cents. Overtime was commonly required but without extra pay. If they got thirsty in rooms that were often too hot, they only had putrid water to drink, giving many of the girls diarrhea—for which relief was a filthy bathroom they could visit at most twice a day. There were no benefits, no vacations, no sick days, and constant pressure to increase output so as to meet the demands of the American buyers.

Another woman, Mahamuda Akter, endured being beaten and slapped, called a "son of a bitch" and her parents denigrated as "whores," all as part of the system of control in another Bangladeshi factory sewing clothing for a major American retailer. In a factory of 4,000 workers, most of whom were young women, she worked over 14 hours a day, and was routinely made to stretch her shift to 19 hours—after which she would sleep at her station until the next shift began a few hours later. At 17 cents an hour, she was unable to save money. As an 18 year old at 79 pounds, she did not expect much beyond her twenties. At age 30 in many such factories, women are no longer hired, being seen as too decrepit to meet production quotas.[1]

What I was coming to understand, through my attempts to track down the homes of my branded products, was that many of us in the United States rely on these women for our clothing, whether functional or fashionable. More than four-fifths of clothing sold in the United States is produced by outside labor. Some of that comes from impoverished Bangladesh, where sewing factories number well over three thousand.[2]

These stories from Bangladesh are overwhelmingly common—and sometimes sound to me like news reports from another planet. A report from the National Labor Committee in 2002 disclosed that Chinese factories that produce toys for American companies are havens of abuse of labor. Toy production often exposes workers to toxic chemicals, such as paints and glues, and factory temperatures top 100 degrees. Naomi Klein's sojourn to the Philippines, which included an illegal foray into a factory making American products, resulted in similar reports. Cramped living conditions, dangerous treks to and from work, bans on pregnancy, reprisals against those who organize unions—all on the backs of teenagers and young adult women. Adolescent girls are the employees of choice for such sweatshops, one activist told Klein, because "they are scared and uneducated about their rights."[3] The needs of their families, and a sense of "patriotism and national duty," means that poor young women around the world are "sent off to sweatshop factories the way a previous generation of young men were sent off to war."[4]

The specifics of the excesses may change from country to country, but the fact of excesses is numbingly clear. There are now more than enough research reports, videos, and testimony from workers to convince any fair-minded consumer that most of us are implicated in an economy whose violence is our business.

My purpose is not to deny all the benefits of American capitalism, and even branding itself, in the last several decades. My books, for example, are sold in part because of the branding power deployed by my publishers, and I do not want to dismantle the relative free enterprise system of public speaking, which is a capitalist circuit that allows me extra income. But I am suggesting that these women workers demand from many of us some soul-searching and some economic self-examination. Their working conditions are the lifeblood of our globalizing economy. This cheap, exhausting, and dangerous labor makes possible our enjoyment of our brands.

The most melancholy irony of our economy is that many of the products assembled by the poor outside the United States are purchased by the poor and lower classes inside the United States. Huge chain department stores often depend on cheaply produced goods to sell to American consumers who demand inexpensive products. This has to be one of the saddest commentaries on our society today—that the middle classes, in order to get the cheapest goods possible, allow themselves to be beneficiaries of an economy in which the poor exploit the poor. A poor American child wearing a cheap logoed T-shirt is a devastating symbol.

HUMAN DIGNITY WITHOUT EXCEPTIONS

Many companies take advantage of consumer indifference to establish plants in Latin America or overseas that denigrate workers. Of course wage and benefit standards should conform to the needs of the particular society—it is not a matter of forcing overseas companies into an American wage system—but what is of concern, especially for an economic spirituality, is a basic standard of human decency. That basic standard of decency will be different in different cultures, but it will never cease to exist in any culture. All humans, regardless of any variable—religion, economic status, race or ethnicity, sex, orientation—are created in the image of God, and thereby deserving of basic decency. Human life does not exist to serve the brand economy. The brand economy should serve human life and flourishing. Wherever it fails to do so, this provocation to people of faith and goodwill demands a response.

A living wage for makers of our branded products is different from a "minimum wage." A living wage is enough to keep a family healthy and allow a basic participation in the life of a society. *What* that living wage is will differ from city to city and from country to country around the world. But *that* there is a living wage in each context is indisputable. The basics of human flourishing, of course, are different from standards of excess or tokens of entitlement. Not everyone really needs a car, fifty different kinds of cereal, or a television to flourish as a human being. Perhaps not even many Americans. But everyone does need a family-supporting wage, basic health care, enough income to save for the future, nutritious food, the ability to organize, and safe living and working conditions. If an employer extracts work from someone at the expense of any of these basic needs, then they are at risk of a minor to a major violation of human rights. Likewise, if an employee takes significant advantage of an employer (through, for example, intentional misreporting of hours worked or through stealing) who is providing these basics, the employee is also culpable for offenses against their fellow workers, because it is reasonable for the employer to try to recover those losses—which will sometimes happen at the cost of the greater good of workers.

In other words, we each already practice an economic spirituality in the work arrangements we support when we support brands—and also in our own local work arrangements.

Of course, even by offering *any* jobs whatsoever, many companies are offering the world's disadvantaged more than they would have had otherwise. Isn't a few cents an hour better than no cents an hour, and a fifteen-hour work day better than none at all? Such an argument presumes that our only choices are to abandon workers or to exploit them. Keeping our corporations accountable does not mean causing more damage to foreign workers by pulling business out of their countries. It means nothing more nor less than treating foreign workers with dignity and decency as far as possible. It is a damning criticism of our society that what should be such an obvious standard for all workers—dignity and decency—is routinely ignored by corporations in part because we the consumers often demand branded goods at the absolute cheapest price possible.

LOGOS UNBOUND

Naomi Klein's discussion of the recent history of the rise of brands is very helpful. She points out important changes in the nature of global corporations that have made the branding economy possible.

Klein reminds us that in the last few decades, global corporations have turned to a few strategies to remain successful: "outsourcing," "downsizing," and "distancing" from commodity production. Outsourcing is hiring an outside contractor to do something the company itself used to do. Downsizing is stripping a company down to its essentials so as to make do with as little as possible, to maximize profits—often hiring temps to do jobs that full-time salaried workers used to perform.

To stay competitive, global corporations are attempting to distance themselves from earthbound issues like workers, wages, unions, and factories. More and more, they turn their focus to the construction of an ethereal brand-image. Their logos must be globally recognizable, symbolizing an attitude, a feeling, a value, or a lifestyle, while avoiding conjuring up any images of the earthly origins of the products that bear the logo. The logo must suggest a certain ethos but not remind the consumer that someone somewhere actually makes the products that bear the logo. The logo should float freely above and beyond the way it was actually produced.

Klein pictures this development as a contest among global companies: "whoever owns the least, has the fewest employees on the payroll and produces the most powerful images, as opposed to products, wins the race." Klein calls this a "race toward weightlessness."[5]

> A select group of corporations ... attempt[s] to free itself from the corporeal world of commodities, manufacturing and products to exist on another plane. Anyone can manufacture a product, they reason. . . . Such menial tasks, therefore, can and should be farmed out to contractors and subcontractors whose only concern is filling the order on time and under budget. . . . Headquarters, meanwhile, is free to focus on the real business at hand—creating a corporate mythology powerful enough to infuse meaning into these raw objects just by signing its name.[6]

Klein goes on to argue that

> after establishing the "soul" of their corporations, the superbrand companies have gone on to rid themselves of their cumbersome bodies, and there is nothing that seems more cumbersome, more loathsomely corporeal, than the factories that produce their products.[7]

Many superbrand corporations own few or none of their own factories today. They contract out to brokers who oversee such gross materiality. "Transcendent meaning machines" practice "corporate transcendence,"[8] separating the brand as an ideal experience or lifestyle from the commodity and its earthly associations—the who, what, when, where, how and why of its production.

DISPOSABLE BODIES

Many of us have had friends or relatives whose manufacturing or management jobs have permanently disappeared, though the products they used to make are alive and well. We now know that many of these jobs are part of patterns of production migrating south or overseas, but we often do not relate this migration to the rise of branding.

Klein thus helpfully links the predominance of the logo with the loss of jobs in North America and the migration of production jobs to the poorest areas of the world. As the brand or logo is elevated by corporations, corporeal bodies (particularly the lesser members) become essentially disposable. The human elbow grease behind the logos, all the sewing, stitching, cutting, gluing, and assembling, cannot compete with the logo for the corporation's attention. The messy cares of the bodies that give these logos material life, such as wages, health care, savings accounts, humane working conditions—whether in the United States or abroad—are finally separated from the brand itself. In this way of doing business, bodies are at best a necessary evil to be dealt with as minimally as possible, with surgical gloves and masks, and only occasionally.

Klein's analysis is of extraordinary importance for all people of good will, and for Christians in particular. What strikes me as a theologian is that there is a remarkable congruence—a disturbing complementarity—between the ascendance of branding and a widespread Christian skepticism about the goodness of the human body. I think that such a dangerous congruence helps make possible Christian apathy about the injustices of our branding economy.

CHRISTIANITY AND
DENIGRATION OF THE BODY

Unfortunately, Christians today are widely perceived as people who are afraid of the fleshiness, the carnality, of the body, often still surprisingly unhealthily secretive about sexuality, skeptical of the spiritual value of physical pleasures, and engaged in a low-intensity war with the physical.

Christian skepticism about the goodness of the human body dates all the way back to the first century of Christian life, and has persisted despite being seen as heretical by important streams of Christianity. But Christian antipathy to the body did not start as an abstract philosophical debate. Instead, it began with debates about the identity of Jesus.

By the late first century, or perhaps even earlier, some Christians were charging that others Christians denied the full humanity of Jesus. People accused of such a denial were soon called "docetists." *Docetism*, simply put, is the denial that Jesus was fully human. Docetists apparently held that Jesus did not really suffer, he did not really eat and drink, and he was not truly a human being in the robust sense in which we commonly think of ourselves as embodied human beings, with emotions, appetites, desires, passions, and bodily limitations. The linguistic root of docetism is the Greek *dokein*, "to seem" (as in Jesus only "seeming" to be human while truly being a divine spirit).

One can quote the Bible to justify seemingly any position, and it is possible to find scriptural evidence for a docetic Christ—which suggests that early docetists weren't making this all up out of nothing. Jesus, after all, often acts like he doesn't have or need a fully human body. He passes through locked doors, walks on water, seems not to need to eat, and often slips, ghostlike, out of sight.[9]

However, many other scriptural passages seem to be pushing back against a growing docetism in the early church. Many scriptures go to some length to highlight Jesus' full humanity and his bodiliness. These scriptures emphasize Jesus' human emotions, the physicality of his eating, the palpable reality of his wounds, or other specific sufferings of his body.[10]

This internal tug-of-war in the New Testament indicates that from very early, many Christians had difficulty accepting Jesus' full humanity. And yet if Jesus were not fully human, a fundamental claim of Christianity—God fully with humanity in the Incarnation—is negated. And if Christians are to claim that salvation is for the whole person, and is not just a matter, for example, of a God accepting our brains, our heads, or some other limited region of our selves, then the mediator for this salvation must be fully human also. (There is a residual "mythological" quality about denying Jesus' humanity—a premodern sort of fascination with gods or spirits roaming the earth.) And if Jesus were not really fully a human body, for Christians that would imply God's definitive judgment against the goodness of the body and seem to reverse the original intrinsic goodness of God's creation, of which embodied humans were the apex, as suggested in the first chapter of Genesis.

But as I noted, docetism is not merely a historical curiosity. It is alive and well today wherever Christians deny Jesus' full humanity or the holiness of their own bodies—as fleshly, as profoundly "of this world."

DENIGRATION OF EMBODIMENT
THROUGH ACTIONS—NOT JUST THOUGHT

I once had a girlfriend who continuously said to me, "I don't put any stock in what you say—I only take what you *do* seriously." This drove me nuts, because she was keen at pointing out contradictions between my professed beliefs (about our relationship, especially) and my actual behavior. Though we broke up (we weren't the right brand for each other), she had an important (if uncomfortable) point. It holds true not just for relationships but for faith.

We have all had the experience that we can say that we believe something, and yet our actions in fact betray our beliefs. In other words, our actions show others what it is we truly believe. Actions disclose that value, idea, commitment, or person to which we have entrusted ourselves. Indeed, our *concepts* find a home in our *living*— not vice versa. What we hold intellectually always has some relationship to how we live our whole lives. That we hold something intellectually in tension with how we actually live is a common experience. It doesn't mean we are ill-intentioned. Sometimes we hold things intellectually because it helps us deal with the way we are actually living. No one should be expected to have *fully* integrated what they believe conceptually with what their free actions declare about their beliefs.

Here we have to dig a little deeper theologically. I want to specifially address those who would like to call themselves Christians. For all other people of goodwill, what follows is meant to help you understand a Christian perspective on economic spirituality. What does it really mean for Christians to accept that Jesus was fully human? Most might say that they "believe" that Jesus was human, much as they would say they believe in God's existence, or they believe in sin or eternal life.

Someone who talks about believing in a generous God of gracious love from whom all creation springs and, yet, whose choices show them to be a person of fear, retribution, and pettiness would rightfully invite a question about what sort of ultimate power they believe in. And likewise, someone who denies God's existence and shuns institutional religion and yet chooses unselfishness, generosity, and faithfulness to others may not intellectually believe in the God of a religious tradition, and yet, in action, they seem to affirm that justice is a transcendental good and gracious love is the final word about our lives—which is precisely what many "institutional" believers mean by God.

So there can be a difference between what we believe as manifest in the *concepts* that we hold verbally, and what we believe as manifest in the way that we *live*.

Thus it only makes sense to acknowledge that it is one thing for Christians to accept Jesus' humanity conceptually, and another to act in everyday life in a way that affirms Jesus' humanity, what could be called a "performative" acceptance.

Let me give another example, from my own tradition, of this difference between belief held conceptually and belief manifest performatively. There is much evidence that young Catholic Christians today are largely illiterate about many of the resources of Catholic tradition, even of such "recent" major events as Vatican II.[11] But when this illiteracy is discussed and fretted over, scholars (and parents) are usually talking about *conceptual* illiteracy. They mourn that young Catholics don't know definitions of sin, grace, the Church, sacraments, or the content of specific prayers.

Yet, as we have just seen, there are other kinds of literacy. Young Catholics, in fact, manifest a *performative* literacy of Vatican II every time they freely *act* so as to endorse key ideas from the Council, such as the Church as the people of God, the value of religious liberty, social justice, or ecumenism. Moreover, this performative literacy does not need to have been inspired exclusively or consciously from the Catholic Church to count as "Catholic." (After all, the Catholic

Church's teachings on each of these issues were not the utterly unique inventions of Catholic tradition, but were assembled through "dialogue" with non-Catholic peoples, culture, and religions.)

BELIEVING IN JESUS' HUMANITY THROUGH CHRISTIANS' EVERYDAY ECONOMIC LIFE

I want to encourage us to pay particular attention to this *performative* belief. In my own faith tradition, Christians often act as if their beliefs about their faith, and their actual economic behavior, can exist on two different planes. Many assert that they can believe in Jesus, then, and more or less conduct their economic relationships according to strictly "secular" (market, business) criteria. But if beliefs are evident not only through what we verbalize, but through how we live, through how we freely "perform" our convictions, then Christians must discard this widespread and misleading attitude about Christian life. As a Christian, what I believe about Jesus—or do not believe— will and must be manifest in the way I use my economic resources.

One important reason that Christians do not take responsibility for the shadow side of our brand economy is that they do not see their economic actions as manifesting their core spiritual beliefs. But we may each look to the way we use our freedom to dignify the human body—our own and others' bodies.

Though few Christians today would say that they are docetists, they are usually thinking only of conceptual docetism. But at least as important is the reality of a "performative" docetism. This latter sort of docetism is a freely chosen style of living by Christians that indicates that they believe that Jesus' humanity is less important than his divinity. A performative docetism would be a freely chosen style of living that hesitates about the incarnation—in other words, that refuses to embrace the *essential* and *good* character of the body, that refuses to embrace the fact that the body influences and mediates every single thing we do, including how we *do* our relation to all that is holy.

Though human bodies may sometimes seem frail, distracting and the source of infinite hindrance, the paradox of the incarnation for Christians is that the "Word becoming flesh" *elevates* human bodiliness by revealing the body to be the privileged place of God's self-disclosure. The human body of Jesus became *the* medium through which God revealed Godself. Jesus did not escape his body to bear God. It was precisely as a fully human person that he revealed God-with-us. Divinity is given to us in and through fully human embodied existence. Christian faith offers that humans can become like Jesus through dignifying the fullness of humanity in ourselves and others—not through escaping our body or our humanness, as ancient and contemporary docetists would like to do. That Jesus was fully human, and in and through that fullness divine, remains one of the most radical teachings in the history of religion; Christians rest uneasily atop an unexploded theological bomb.

DOCETISM AND OUR ECONOMY

Christians have been, and are often still, docetic in everyday living, performatively. Because economics are part of our everyday lives, Christians can very easily slip into economic docetism. By economic docetism, I mean Christian participation in the economy that denies the facticity, holiness, and potential revelatory character of our bodiliness or the bodiliness of others. I mean Christian participation in the economy that denies the body as *the* existential locus of our sufferings and pleasures, our human dignity, the fullness of our humanity. In short, economic docetism is the use of economics to abbreviate our living of our full humanity, in all its complexity, richness, and ambiguity. This often occurs today through a denial that the body is essential to human flourishing, and a presumption that the sufferings and pleasures of some bodies (such as Bangladeshi women) are *less important* than others (such as American middle-class consumers).

Docetism, whether conceptual or performative, is not new. It is perhaps the most persistent cancer on faith in Christian life for twenty centuries. What *is* new is that economic docetism takes novel forms in the twenty-first century: separating a branded product from the human, bodily, earthly locations of the product's production.

Economic docetism tempts Christians to agree with the president of one branding agency who traded on a body-spirit separation when he proposed that "Products are made in the factory, but brands are made in the mind."[12] Similarly, another brand manager argued that the brand as "intangible asset . . . is clearly recognized as a company's most valuable asset"—leaving one to wonder what the company thinks of its employees.[13] In the pithy expression of one author of a book on branding, "What isn't matter is what matters."[14]

Yet as we have seen, Christians—in order to become Christians—must resist the "corporate transcendence" of the branding economy becoming a temptation to docetic "corporeal transcendence." Concern for the human flourishing of others, especially those who are different, is part of the costly grace that allows Christians to call themselves by that name, and to stop defaming the name of Jesus by reducing him to an American middle-class morality that is too purposefully busy and cautious to consider the well-being of others' bodies as important as their own.

Still, it must be asked whether Jesus' bodiliness is *enough* to inspire and empower people of my own faith tradition to a more mature economic spirituality.

While a performative expression of belief in Jesus' humanity is possible and necessary for Christians, why are so many Christians deeply conflicted about the body, and hesitant about economic spirituality—despite Jesus' presence at the heart of both? To answer this question, we are going to have to lay some of the blame on the scriptures themselves. We have to look at how scripture presents the body.

CHAPTER 5

ECONOMIC SPIRITUALITY:

STARTING WITH THE BODY

Like many Catholics, as a child, I frequently daydreamed my way through the scripture readings at mass. Often the preaching had nothing to do with these readings, thus they seemed to be part of some ritualistic recitation of family tradition that was not meant to be questioned but endured. Most Catholics today, I venture, still cannot tell you what "the readings" were about an hour after mass. Still, that many Independence, Missouri, Catholics sat together quietly for a while most weekends is itself important in forming community.

However, when I was an altar boy at St. Mark's (1978–1982), I felt some duty to pay attention to the scriptures being read, like the way I always had to know the count and the location of the baserunners in those days when I played center field. So I do remember hearing a particular phrase once in a while at mass: "the body of Christ." It would usually come up in the second reading, which was often from the apostle Paul's letters.

Paul would tell people that they were a part of the body of Christ (a heady philosophical claim for a 10 year old), Paul kvetched over people dividing the body of Christ, and he talked about the different functions of the body's "members" (I never got the pun until graduate school).

I suppose I owe it to my laser-beam altar boy concentration that I remember our priests preaching about the body of Christ as the Catholic Church—or sometimes as all Christian churches. Of course I simply thought these good priests were telling me what Paul really meant. When I was a child, I understood Paul in a childish way. Now, however, I have to deal with him—and the body of Christ—as an adult.

And I have to do so because this important teaching contributes to Christian apathy. Paul often imagines the body of Christ as a community of Christians, more or less separate from other communities. But this idea has often encouraged Christians to be a self-enclosed group; it has sometimes kept Christians from seeing the larger world as their "body," also, and thus from taking economic responsibility for that body. This is not a matter of liking or disliking Paul. It is a matter of asking whether Christians, precisely *as* part of Christ's body, are separate from or bound up with the well-being of all other people.

THE BODY OF CHRIST

In his letters collected in the Christian scriptures, Paul uses the concept of the "body of Christ" to symbolize the way in which Christians are unified while retaining their unique diversity. Each has their own unique gifts to put to use for the larger Christian community, and we need only locate ourselves as the foot, hand, or eye and we will be able to live in harmony with the other members of Christ's body. Thus, we will not try to do another's function, nor keep from doing our own seeing, grasping, or walking while serving the larger body. The body of Christ is a thoroughly communal concept. Members are not defined in and through themselves, but as members of a more fundamental community, Christ's body.[1] Being appended to Christ attaches Christians to each other. Paul writes that "We, who are many, are one body in Christ, and individually we are members one of another" (Romans 12:5).

Because this unity of Christians across time and place happens through a shared faith in the God of Jesus, tradition often calls this the "mystical body" of Christ, signifying the deep mystery of Christians' connections to each other across history and culture.

For Paul, baptism is the foundational incorporation into Christ's body: "In the one Spirit we were all baptized into one body" (1 Corinthians 12:13). The eucharist is a source in daily experience for further incorporation. "Because there is one bread, we who are many are one body, for we all partake of the one bread" (1 Corinthians 10:17).

A SELF-CONTAINED BODY

Paul, like any of us, had his own assumptions about bodies when he wrote about the "body" of Christ. As I suggested in chapter 3, our imaginations always influence how we see the world, and how we organize what we take in. Paul, like many of us, imagined the body in a particular way. He imagined that a body is a well-bounded thing, like a fenced-in yard, with obvious and clear borders. Even when talking about a spiritual body of Christ, he (like anyone) had to start with his own imagining of what makes a human body a body.

Taking one's point of departure from these passages in Paul naturally leads Christians to think that being responsible to the "body" of Christ means caring for this body's members, so that the whole body will function well.

This is quite understandable, because it seems self-evident that despite its many members, the human body has clear boundaries that make it "one" body, integrated and whole. Our bodies are bounded by the flesh as a self-contained organism, with different members functioning in harmony. In much Christian literature and preaching, these members are imagined like those in Paul's examples, such as head, hands, and feet. These members help demarcate the body's surface. They form a boundary with the world by distinguishing the body from the world. These members are also clearly visible to the eye. On this model of the body, even when the Christian community—as "the body of Christ"—cares for the world, it is as if Christ's well-functioning body ambles toward or stoops down to embrace those in need. The one body of Christ, Christians often imagine, cares for what is *not* a part of this body.

I doubt that this way of imagining the body of Christ does justice to what bodies are, and how we experience our bodies. In other words, I think this notion of the body needs to be reimagined, and I will sketch a different imagining of it shortly.

Though Paul may never have intended it, his model of the self-enclosed body may contribute to what I earlier called economic docetism. How? Because once we imagine "the world" as outside of the "body" of Christ, we then create a problem for ourselves regarding how the "world" relates to Christ's "body," or how the "secular" relates to the "spiritual." This then creates plenty of space for Christians to opt out of responsibility for "the world," for thinking that economic resources and faith (relating "to the world" and relating "to Christ") are two utterly separate realms.

In other words, Christians' thinking about the body creates a false problem, which we then spend inordinate amounts of time trying to solve: How ought Christians relate to the world as members of Christ's body? But, like many of our spiritual quandaries, this is a problem *we* have created, and that we can try to think our way through . . . especially by backing out of the presuppositions that set up the problem in the first place.

There are indeed ways of getting around this problem. What if the "world" is already within the "body"? If that is the case, then caring for the body is never separate from caring for the world on which the body depends.

We have to try to forget our traditional assumptions about the body, to defamiliarize the body, to think about it in new ways. We have to re-ask the question: How is it that Christians come to know themselves as part of Christ's body? Yes, through baptism and eucharist. However, I think there is another source for an experiential knowing of what it means to participate in Christ's body. That source is our own lived embodiment.

The body, of course, is interpreted in and through Christ in Paul's theology. But let us take Paul very seriously by using his own term—*body*—and asking what it really means. After all, the body for Paul is a key metaphor for Christian identity. Can we construe the metaphor in a way that does not encourage economic docetism?

WE ARE OUR BODIES

When Paul writes about the body of Christ, he appeals to his audience's own experience of their bodies to demonstrate his claim: "*Just as* the body is one and has many members . . . *so it is* with Christ" (1 Corinthians 12:12). Paul's claim would have been utterly unpersuasive if his hearers did not experience their own bodies as singular yet plural—as several limbs and appendages somehow unified in one body. In other words, Paul knew that only after we know what it means to *be* embodied can we meaningfully interpret the concept of the body of Christ and its implications for Christian discipleship.

The field of philosophy that tries to describe the basics of embodiment is called phenomenology. Whenever we think carefully about the essence of our body's feeling, perceiving, sensing, moving—and attempt to describe it—we are thinking "phenomenologically." By that, I mean we are looking closely at the basic "phenomena" or data of our everyday experience—how we encounter the world before we interpret the world.

One important contemporary phenomenologist is Drew Leder, trained both as a physician and philosopher. Leder's book *The Absent Body* is a friendly but critical conversation with the work of a famous twentieth-century French phenomenologist, Maurice Merleau-Ponty. For all people seeking a more mature spirituality, and in a special way for Christians, the nature of their conversation is important for understanding the body and its relation to our spirituality.

Both Leder and Merleau-Ponty think that philosophy has too often forgotten the simplest "fact" of our being: that our humanity subsists in our being embodied people, instead of just "minds" or "spirits." But both philosophers realize that thinking about our bodies can be a subtle way of distancing ourselves from our embodiment. We often talk about being embodied as if our bodies were things "out there," and not that which belongs to us more intimately than almost anything else.

For both of these philosophers, we do not *have* bodies, we *are* our bodies. We think, experience, perceive, love, practice faith, relate to others—all this, only in and through our fleshliness. Though I have had a few professors who seemed to live only from the neck up, no one is a disembodied mind, no one pure spirit.

The body, in Leder's careful formulation, is an "unthematized substratum from which the world is acted upon. This transitive nature of the body is essential, inherent, a corporeal primitive."[2] Of course if you have traveled much (or read *National Geographic*), you know that people attach meaning to their bodies very differently in different cultures. Leder does admit "large individual and cultural variations" in the uses and interpretations of different parts of the body. Yet I think he is right that all human bodies share basic commonalities. Cultural "variations are possible only within, and are limited by, the common structure of the human body. Its sensory organs, its forward-directedness, its muscular capacities, are prearticulations upon which all cultures must build."[3]

THE BODY: DEPENDENT ON THE WORLD

But Leder stakes out some differences with Merleau-Ponty about how we should describe our bodies. Leder argues that there was a tendency in the writings of the famous phenomenologist to focus on the body as an organism that *perceives* the world. Leder argues that Merleau-Ponty made perception the key to embodiment.

Given this attention to perception, Merleau-Ponty focused on the *flesh* as the key to thinking about embodiment.[4] Merleau-Ponty's work thus tended to examine perception by careful description of the way bodily surfaces help us perceive through vision and movement.

Leder complements Merleau-Ponty's approach by showing how bodily surfaces are not just *present* to our conscious experience, but also *absent* from it. If you think about it, our bodily surfaces "absent" themselves continually. When we use our bodily surfaces, or even tools that we use as bodily extensions (like spatulas or hammers), they become *absent* to us as they move outward toward their project. When using my fingers or a pick to pluck a bass guitar, for example, I am usually not focusing on the sensations in my hand and fingers. When a skilled carpenter uses a hammer, his focus is on the hammer as an extended limb—so the carpenter can make subtle use of a hammer to nudge, tap, or pound, all with the carpenter's intention invested in the tool, not the hand holding the tool (which becomes "absent" to his or her focus). Leder calls this an "active" sort of absence.

There is also a more "passive" sort of absence that the rest of our bodily surface registers when it is not employed outward in service of a bodily project. For example, when eating, we usually don't think about our feet—they are "passively" absent in contrast to our "actively" absent hands using fork and knife.

In addition to enriching Merleau-Ponty's notion of the perceiving body and its surfaces, Leder explores regions of the body generally left unexplored by Merleau-Ponty. He finds that such regions as our lungs, kidneys, liver, and spleen—our "viscera"—also manifest their own kinds of presence and absence. The basic presences of our viscera in everyday life—breathing (our lungs making themselves present) or eating (our stomach "presencing"), for example—are part of processes that are almost entirely absent from our ability to observe them, to feel them clearly, or to control them. For example, we cannot typically observe, carefully feel, or control well our lungs or stomach in breathing or eating. Whereas Merleau-Ponty often discusses the body in terms of flesh, the visible body, Leder emphasizes "flesh and blood"—the visible *and* visceral body. The body entire is "one thing."[5]

So what difference does it make how we think of the body? Leder's phenomenology of the body goes right to the heart of one of the most important spiritual issues: the relationship of the body to the larger world.

Leder argues that, for Merleau-Ponty, the body perceives the world through the flesh. There is a distinct boundary between the body and the world. Leder, on the other hand, seeing the body as "flesh *and* blood," imagines a different relationship: the world is profoundly *inside* the body; the body is immersed in the world. The boundary between the two is only apparent; it is never fixed, never clear. Leder writes that his body is

> sustained through a . . . "blood" relation with the world. It is installed within me, not just encountered from without. The inanimate, calcified world supports my flesh from within in the form of bones. A world of organic, autonomous powers circulates within my visceral depths. Science tells me that some ten quadrillion bacteria live within my body. I cannot even claim my own cells fully as my own. In all probability, they evolved out of symbiotic relations between different prokaryotic cells, one living inside another. My body everywhere bears the imprint of Otherness.
>
> This encroachment of the world is renewed at every moment by visceral exchanges with the environment. In sleep I give myself over to anonymous breathing, relinquishing the separative nature of distance perception. Even waking perception is ultimately in service to the visceral. In the most basic sense, the animal looks around to find things to eat and avoid being eaten. . . . As I eat, the thickness of the flesh that separates self from world melts away. No longer perceived across a distance, *the world dissolves into my own blood*, sustaining me from within via its nutritive powers. I am not just a gazing upon the world but one who feeds on it, drinks of it, breathes it in.[6]

Even adult bodies are like the bodies of infants, utterly dependent on a surrounding world, absorbing from and expelling into that world. The body is not a closed system but an open one, utterly reliant on the world, which is always "installed within" the body.

If Leder is right about the nature of the body, then when Christians claim to be part of the "body of Christ," they must admit the importance of the world's well-being for the well-being of the body of Christ. Many modern interpretations of the body of Christ, drawing on some Pauline texts, tend to be "flesh"-based interpretations, emphasizing bodily surface metaphors, like Christians as Christ's hands, feet, or arms. Turning to a "flesh and blood" body that recognizes that world and body are deeply entwined blocks docetic uses of the concept "body of Christ"—uses that keep Christians from being fully involved in, and taking appropriate responsibility for, the human joys and hopes—and economics—of the larger world.

The body itself always incorporates the world. The body *is* body only by receiving others; it lives only with vital reference to an embryonic and fetal life, to the body of a mother, to the genes of its parents.[7] The body is essentially open, not closed. Leder writes that

> My ecstatic flesh opens onto, mirrors the surrounding world of other bodies. *I am not then simply an "I" but all that I am not, a perspective upon the universe as a whole.* Similarly, as "blood" . . . I find a consanguinity with processes that far outrun the traditional boundaries of self. It is not "I" as conscious, limited thing, that first gave rise to or sustain my self, but a wider context of natural powers of which I am but a partial expression.[8]

The body of Christ cannot only be imagined on the model of a self-enclosed corpus that is constituted by surface regions such as eye, ear, foot. The body of Christ, if it is truly thought through the lived body, is a body dependent upon absent regions and processes we cannot control, but that themselves implicate us with the world. There is no clear body/world separation. The body of Christ, as a *body*, only "lives" because it is dependent on "outside" processes and resources that this body cannot consciously control, but to which it is indebted. The body of Christ is obligated to the world.

Leder writes that for the body, "each breath speaks of my dependency upon the whole."[9] "The body itself proclaims spirit in our lives, that is, transcendence, mystery, and interconnection."[10] "I gaze up at the stars . . . at the same time I know that the carbon molecules from which my body is made were forged in the furnace of dying stars. I am thus doubly connected to even the far reaches of the universe."[11]

THE BODY: CAUGHT UP IN
NATURE AND CULTURE

Almost all of Leder's examples of the body's dependence on the world are drawn from nature. But we could just as well draw from our economy. Then we might think like this:

I gaze down at my brands: shoes, jeans, shirts, gadgets, toys . . . at the same time I know that the materials that enable my comfort were forged under fluorescent lights in a large room of young women half a world away. I am thus doubly connected to even the far reaches of this planet. Those who make the stuff of my world that I use and find pleasure and comfort in, in a way different from the stars, are already a part of me. Economic spirituality means fulfilling my part of my economic relationship with my global neighbor, the one who is part of the world on which my material or even religious body depends.

I must open myself to seeing my goods as part of "one body," and looking through my "goods" to their human producers, assemblers. The body of Christ is thus deeply intertwined with all of nature that is *not* this body, and with the other human cultures that *clothe, feed, and entertain* this body.

The Jewish philosopher Emmanuel Levinas wrote of the importance of the experience not only of "being-in-one's-skin," but of "having-the-other-in-one's-skin."[12] Having the other as one's kin. *Because* we will wear and eat the branded world—we owe the workers of the branded world. Our economy makes us responsible to powers and peoples we did not create and without whom we cannot live.

Levinas wrote that "one comes not into the world but into question."[13] That is to say, we do not come into the world as our personal birthright. The brand economy is not our individual playspace. To be human in the world is to question whether our spiritual and economic practices are taking up the spiritual or economic spaces of others.

In striving to love those who make our branded goods, our sense of self is enlarged. It is an expansion of self that is not finally selfish. In

accounting for the needs of my absent neighbors, I allow love to dis-
tribute my sense of self into global relationships, and thus to be more
appropriately spacious. In so doing, my sense of accountability to the
world changes. In becoming more spacious, I paradoxically achieve
myself more fully, as I become more fully the communal being that I
have always been, but heretofore resisted. I allow love to "expand
me," in the words of psychoanalyst Julia Kristeva, "to the dimensions
of the universe."

CHAPTER 6

THE CHALLENGE OF A MATURING ECONOMIC SPIRITUALITY

I had just come home from viewing the movie *About Schmidt*, starring Jack Nicholson. The film lovingly recounts a middle-aged man's attempt to recover from the death of his wife, and the confrontation with his long-smothered emotions released by her passing. In his lethargy and moody overreliance on his daughter, and his grudging acceptance of her mullet-haired Midwestern fiancé, *About Schmidt* was sweetly unassuming and as "real" as any Hollywood movie I had seen for a long time. Schmidt wrestles with his newly discovered subterranean emotional landscape by writing letters to a needy African boy he discovers through a television ad. These letters to this boy, named Ndugu, become the occasion for Schmidt's awkward inventory of his regrets and consolations as a widower, retired businessman, and father-in-law-to-be.

I returned home to find the movie on the front page of the *New York Times*.[1] I learned that the boy in the movie is actually a real African boy named Abdallah Mtulu, whose family lives in poverty in Tanzania. Though one of the film's publicists became aware of Abdallah by sponsoring him through an international relief organization, neither he nor his family had received any benefits from the production studio in return for the boy's picture and neediness being used throughout the film. (Abdallah's parents gave the studio permission to use their son's picture.)

Our economy in miniature: a product entertaining and pleasurable, whose production depended on the disregard for the dignity of its secret star. The movie company shared the assumption of so many jean, T-shirt, shoe, and coffee maker: that the public has neither the will nor the means to find out about the bodies behind the brands. Were it not for the *Times* reporter, Marc Lacey, would the public have known of Mtulu?

What had my $10 movie ticket funded? The pocketbooks of the production company and Mr. Nicholson, to be sure. But more importantly, my money also endorsed an economic style, a distribution of resources that is not consistent with who I want to be.

But what could I possibly do after the fact? I have as little direct influence over how Hollywood films are made as I do over how my jeans are produced. Is feeling helpless regret enough? Can I fashion my purchases in any way that would be meaningful? Is there *anything* I can do to be more responsible in my economic relationships, toward a maturing economic spirituality? These questions are unavoidable for all people of faith, and as I have tried to show, for the Christian tradition in particular. The way we spend our money is an expression of our faith. Every purchase is as powerful an endorsement or negation of faith in God as any prayer, promise, or creed.

THE ECONOMY SEEMS
BEYOND OUR CONTROL

Younger generations live in a world that appears to many as irreversibly ambiguous, an admixture exploitation and generosity, getting ahead and giving up, dysfunction and desire, power and peace, depression and delight, rage and recalcitrance. Our imaginations are filled with the soft pornography of movies and the sweet visage of the Pope or Dalai Lama. We live with a taste for intensity and ecstasy, and a temptation toward addiction. We live with the knowledge and helpless feeling that someone somewhere may be suffering because of the way that the coffee we savor or the clothes we enjoy are produced, and we are too busy, tired, or already have enough of our own "issues" to even begin to do anything about it.

We live with the suspicion that every preacher, politician, and parent may well be deceiving us or themselves, and yet we live with the need to deeply trust them. We are neither romantic nor well-educated about our American past. We will volunteer in charity but are skeptical about what gets called justice. We know that being psychologically healthy is important and we know that an overfocus on it can make us self-absorbed.

We want some guidelines, we want some structure, but we know that for some parts of our lives it is too late, and we don't know what to do with those parts of our lives. We don't want to be judged by others and want to refrain from judging others, yet we also wish that someone would stand up confidently and make some clear judgments about difficult issues. For the most part, we're not going to fight you about whether there is one true religion, one true sexual identity, one true way of being family. "Who can know for sure?" And "Who am I to judge?" we ask, wanting secretly to know more surely and judge more confidently.

We know that changing "the system" is both absolutely necessary and utterly impossible, whether it be religion, politics, or the economy. These systems seem beyond our ability to upend.

The post-1960s generations are neither the first nor the only generations to be skeptical of overturning the system. What is unique to us is the setting that brings us to these convictions—especially the influence of corporate branding in a global economy on our everyday life and faith. What is also unique today is the way our ambiguity about the economy is expressed: in a resigned if uneasy accommodation, a détente, with branding in particular and consumer culture in general.

Sara Jewett, at the time a senior at Duke University, was interviewed by *Rolling Stone* during a trip to Nicaragua to observe sweatshops. Jewett said, "I think, deep down, a lot of us feel that America's consumer culture isn't entirely right, that there's a spiritual deadening that's come with it." The reporter, Katherine Marsh, notes that for Jewett, "consumer culture is not entirely right, but she implies it's not entirely wrong either. Hers is an activism of accommodation." Marsh quotes Jewett: "I think one of the legacies of Sixties activism is that the older generation expects you to choose one system or another. Our generation has really rejected the idea that your choices must be mutually exclusive."[2]

The inescapability of our economy's cool rationality is also expressed in the 2000 song "Optimistic" by Radiohead.

> *The big fish eat the little ones, the big fish eat the little ones*
> *Not my problem, give me some*
> *You can try the best you can, you can try the best you can*
> *The best you can is good enough*[3]

The message is humane and pragmatic in the face of a resigned accommodation. The economy seems like a law of nature, in this song, and not a human arrangement.

Interestingly, Naomi Klein reported that one 1995 study "found that a majority of Missouri high school students who watched Channel One's mix of news and ads in their classrooms thought that sports stars paid companies to be in their commercials." As one ninth-grade girl said, "I don't know why athletes do that—pay all that money for all them ignorant commercials for themselves. Guess it makes everyone like 'em more and like their teams more." For the study's designer, "the comment demonstrates a disturbing lack of media literacy, proof positive that kids can't critically evaluate the advertising they see on television."

But as Klein argues, perhaps some youth have intuited a deeper truth, "that sponsorship is a far more complicated process than the buyer/seller dichotomy that existed in previous decades, [and] to talk of who sold out or bought in has become impossibly anachronistic." This cohort may be expected to sense the contemporary branding culture, because they are the ones who, more than any of us, "grew up sold."[4]

In such a climate, how can one speak meaningfully of creative resistance to branding's underside through an economic spirituality?

Is resistance not an outmoded facet of a faithful life, better suited perhaps for the World War II days of Dietrich Bonhoeffer, because in such a war one can presumably gain a more heightened and refined sense of the cost of discipleship (or at least we fantasize as much)? Or is resistance better suited for the '60s generation, who so often were invigorated by the conviction that military, racial or gender systems could be undermined, undone, broken, collapsed, overturned?

Instead of modeling resistance on the apocalyptic overturning of an institution, a structure, or a system in the short term, I turn to the Jesus of Luke 8:15 to provide a principle for realistic hope: "When [you] hear the word, hold it fast in an honest and good heart, and bear fruit with *patient endurance.*" This is indeed good news for generations who think that when it comes to grasping the complexities of their enmeshment in the global economy, or taking faithful action in response to it, little meaningful work can be done.

TWO APPROACHES TO A MATURING ECONOMIC SPIRITUALITY

Because I am concerned with how faith communities can sponsor attention to branding, I will suggest some practical ways forward, ways that also may be used and adapted by people with no explicit religious affiliation.

There are, then, at least two routes to a maturing economic spirituality: the *direct* and the *indirect*.

Directly taking on economic spirituality in ministry seems to have both advantages and disadvantages. On the one hand, direct approaches can emulate the prophets by confronting people directly with a faith-based imperative of changing our economic ways. Many people are thirsty for such a challenge to their everyday ways and eager to hear alternative vistas announced. Isaiah and Amos may live again in our words whenever we name concrete and specific ways in which contemporary economic life betrays our obligation to our economic relationships. On the other hand, absent concrete alternatives, without definite ways of buying products differently, and sometimes even *with* them, the direct approach can lapse into a moralizing and self-righteous pseudoprophetic preaching that most of us abhor and yet many of us lapse into. A fresh countercultural temperament has a way of creating not only new prophets but also some very cloying preachers.

Aware of this tendency in myself, and enduring it in others, I advocate an indirect approach alongside a direct one. By indirection, I mean practices that are not so much didactic as elliptical in their pedagogy about economic spirituality. Here ministry aims not to deal with the end result of economics in everyday life, such as which products ought one to purchase and why, but with the patterns of life that occur many steps before such purchases are ever made, and create the conditions of mind and heart that make such purchases seem necessary. While indirection can seem a waste of time and evince a lack of faith in the short run because it is not directly intervening in the economic forces of the present, in the long run, indirect efforts may be the most prophetic approach.

INDIRECT APPROACHES

Economic spirituality is fostered indirectly in several ways:

• People can be encouraged to accept the mysterious depth of their human identity, the irreplaceable uniqueness of their own dignity.

But "human dignity" and "mystery" can easily ossify into buzzwords. We continually have to find evocative ways of describing dignity and mystery. I propose that we ask ourselves what is that undomesticatable region of ourselves that cannot be bought, cannot be branded? What about us cannot be traded away, drugged up, or dieted off? What about ourselves cannot be sold, sweated away, or co-opted by an advertiser? How would you describe that dimension of yourself, and what might it mean to live from that "place" in your economic life?

• Christians in particular can be vigilant about the economic enmeshment of the Church's own spiritual practices.

We can be suspicious of the idea that God's grace is a set of coins stored in a chest that the Church may give out when someone practices piety, coins that will eventually purchase heaven. We can question the idea that grace is one person's private property. We can doubt the notion that there are purely "Christian" practices that have escaped influencing and being influenced by the economy.

Most prophetically today, we may protest the equating of divine blessing with material wealth, with sales of Christian books, with big attendance figures in ministry, or with fawning media attention. Ignatius, recovering from health problems, arrived at a Spanish hospice and began a ministry of Christian education for children. Ignatius later related that his "brother strongly objected to this, saying that no one would come." Ignatius, however, "replied that one would be enough."[5] Ignatius practiced a virtue that is of supreme importance for ministry in today's economy: spiritual indifference to numbers. His example reminds us not to reduce the justification for ministry to a quantitative measure, subject inordinately to consumer norms.

Even the way most churches solicit money—tithing—is suspect. Most practice a "don't ask, don't tell" tithing. This is the common practice of asking for money from churchgoers, without questioning how that money was acquired. Was it earned as a result of exploited labor, of morally questionable investments, of tax evasion, or from cheating an employer? Most churches create a silent compromise with their members once the collection plate is passed: We won't ask you, you won't tell us, and both of us will meet our budgetary needs. I hasten to add that this does not mean only perfect people should solicit or give money to churches. The Christian Church would in that case expire almost immediately. I do mean that we can provoke much more adult questions about this tithing practice than we currently do.

We can further question how the church imitates the labor-exploiting tendencies of our economy when we exploit church workers when we have the resources to do otherwise, workers who are assumed to be the ultimate maximizers of their own utility while often serving severely underpaid.

Finally, we can correct a lack of questioning about where ministry resources are produced or manufactured (e.g., the coffee in the ubiquitous church coffee pots, often grown and harvested by farmers whose first world employers refuse to conform to fair trade standards).

The goal of ministry here should be to get itself into a position where it can credibly criticize economic practices in the larger economy. It is telling that one of the most prophetic criticisms of this economy came from Federal Reserve Chairman Alan Greenspan in 2002. He famously described corporate America as sodden with "infectious greed."[6] It is difficult to think of many leaders in American Christianity who levy criticisms with as much credibility.

• We can undertake media fasts.

This requires supporting each other in giving up television, the Internet, or some other media technology, for a specific amount of time. This aids us spiritually by encouraging a critical distance from them, and the brands they mediate, allowing us to check their influence on our imaginations.

Many commentators have noted the extraordinary power of the visual in the branding economy, because that economy depends so heavily on electronic media: magazines, billboards, television, movies, and all manner of visual advertising. Those who work with young adults know of the practical visual literacy that exists among them, sometimes at the expense of verbal or conceptual literacy. We can sometimes recognize logos or media stars more confidently than we can work through concepts or verbal tangles.

Fascinatingly, the philosopher and physician Drew Leder argues that "It is precisely *visual* experience that lends itself most to an experience of disembodiment."[7] Our seeing typically makes us less conscious of our bodies, not more, and does not obviously affect what we are seeing. This is very different from our experience of touch, which usually makes us aware of what our body is doing, and which affects or is affected by our touch. Sight is also the one sense that allows us to engage the world from afar. You don't have to get "involved" in the world to see it. In other words, an intensely visual culture fosters the (mis)conception that we are disembodied people. This is a dangerous temptation for Christians who are already uneasy about Jesus living, dying, and rising as a fully human Jewish man.

And yet Jesus himself often fasted from the "media" of his day. He did this through "toggling." I take the metaphor of toggling from the computer world on which so much of our branded economy depends. To "toggle" is to move fluidly back and forth between various programs on your computer desktop, from the word processor to the calculator to the spreadsheet to a video game to the web browser to email. Those who can toggle successfully are able to allow many different tasks to be "in process" at the same time, though they are giving their attention to only one task at a time.

By toggling spiritually, I mean moving back and forth regularly between the active and the contemplative life. I often think of Jesus as our primary Christian example of someone who knew how to toggle well. In scripture, Jesus is constantly being called out of prayer to take on the world, a rhythm of solitude and solicitude, retreat and return, reflection and reengagement. Between the end of Matthew chapter 7, where Jesus is teaching the crowds, and the beginning of chapter 8, for example, Jesus has mysteriously taken himself away for some private retreat time, so that in 8:1 the text abruptly announces, "When Jesus had come down from the mountain"—followed by the reason he had needed to get away to the mountain in the first place: "great crowds followed him."

Later in that chapter, we see again this toggling in action, as we read "when Jesus saw great crowds around him, he gave orders to go over to the other side"—that is, the eastern side of the sea of Galilee. Matthew decides not to comment on Jesus' retreat, but Jesus' plans are immediately interrupted by a pious scribe who pledges to Jesus, "Teacher, I will follow you wherever you go." I think that what we have here is an unguarded moment, with Jesus' solitude being delayed yet again by a worldly demand—and this time from someone gushing an unswerving loyalty (they must have been the most difficult to deal with). Of course the scribe wouldn't be able to follow wherever Jesus goes, as Jesus had learned time and again, and anyway, right then Jesus just wanted to get away.

These toggling actions of Jesus—coming down from the mountain to great crowds, going away from great crowds to the far shore—are given poignant expression by Jesus a few verses later, and we can hear the lament in his voice: "Foxes have holes, and birds of the air have nests; but [insert frustrated expletive here] the Son of Man has nowhere to lay his head." The familiarity of the text barely conceals the frustrated, and perhaps even a tad resentful, complaint of a man who himself is struggling with how to toggle well.

- The Church can reclaim its role as sponsor of the arts.

The Church can complement the consumption of branded products by providing resources to encourage young people to create and interpret their own cultural products. I know of one church that was planning to construct a recording studio to be used by any young people in the city. Young musicians may use this studio without taking an orthodoxy test. They are simply welcome to create their own forms of culture under the aegis of the church. It is a marvelous example of the church at the service of the world. Contemporary U.S. Christianity has often surrendered this once-great role of the medieval European churches, as patron of the arts.

DIRECT APPROACHES

In contrast to indirect approaches to economic spirituality, direct engagements foster mature decision making in faith about the distribution and use of one's personal and communal resources. Economic spirituality is more directly encouraged through various practices:

- We can practice discernment about our economic decisions.

This discernment begins with asking ourselves, How am I using my economic resources? Who or what am I actually supporting when I purchase certain products? The hard work of answering such questions may only come through taking up a fashion inventory, investigating where each article of clothing you are wearing was manufactured. At each stage, ask: Who did the work? Were living wages paid? Were safe working conditions present? Were unions allowed? Overall, what supports or threats to human dignity were part of the production of your goods? And once you know, what steps will you take to honor your deepened economic spirituality?

- We can draw up declarations of spiritual freedom for our culture, for individuals, families, or communities. I have experimented with the following ten commitments for such declarations in various church ministries:

1. Dignity. We will embody the dignity of all life as our most basic value by nurturing and protecting human life at all stages of the life cycle, and honoring the created goodness of animals and nature.
2. Stewardship. We will live stewardship of life as our fundamental spiritual practice by regularly taking an honest measure of our life resources, offering a portion to the Church or the world.
3. Solidarity. We will allow the impact of our spending on the poorest and most disadvantaged members of society to influence strongly our purchasing habits. We will inquire into the labor practices of companies we patronize and let businesses know, through our words and deeds, that just wages and working conditions for all laborers are non-negotiable matters to people of faith and good will.
4. Community. We will share in co-responsibility for our lives and the lives of others by being accountable to at least one community or family for whom we will be actively present.
5. Toggling. We will craft our schedules by striving for a balanced life, toggling between the active and contemplative modes of solitude, community, recreation, and work.
6. Play. Because all good recreation immerses us in the goodness of all creation, we will make play a priority, both in the form of playful activities and in our taste for the comic dimension of everyday life.

7. Literacy. We will prepare ourselves to transform responsibly our cultures and communities by gaining literacy in our traditions and fluency in our histories.
8. Local culture. We will be creators as well as consumers of culture, supporting local and indigenous popular culture and interpreting all forms of culture through the lenses of faith.
9. Discernment. We will practice ways of being attentive to the presence of God in the world, alive to the absolute uniqueness of our own giftedness, and careful to make moral judgments through an informed conscience.
10. Disattachment. Knowing that there is no lasting spiritual growth without disattachment from material goods, we strive to avoid getting entangled in material goods by avoiding the extremes of overvaluing them and hating them. We will regularly reassess our relationship to our material goods.

Such declarations can be used to orient retreats, worship, religious education, or prayer. But regardless of which commitments orient your own economic spirituality, for many in the post-1960s generations, these practical commitments will have to be undertaken in small steps, supported by a community aware of its own sinfulness, and without the expectation that everything can change overnight.

THE SEDUCTION OF ENTITLEMENT

Growing into a robust and responsible economic spirituality is one of the most necessary yet difficult tasks today for people of faith. One reason we find it so difficult is that our economy has schooled us in entitlement, an attitude that has come to influence almost every relationship in our lives, between students and teachers, children and parents, employees and employers, congregants and clergy.

The brand economy has taught many of us that we deserve the products we want, when we want them, at a price that comports with our needs, and with an image customized for us. Sometimes our entitlement makes us think that others must win us over or prove their worthiness just as a product would through branding. At other times we show that we have internalized the dynamics of corporate branding, asserting a right to market ourselves and achieve recognition our own brand identity by demanding attention, access, or status before we have truly earned it.

Entitlement is an "I am owed" that is rarely verbalized, an impatience when our world cannot be customized, a sense that my style privileges imply spiritual or political privileges in everyday life. Alissa Quart quotes one rabbi, a veteran of bar and bat mitzvahs, who is convinced that "There's a cult of special-ness in the American middle class. Kids have to be special, the party has to be special, and then the families are unwittingly a partner in a communal narcissism, believing that they or their children *own* the ceremony. It's *God's* service."[8] Researchers even talk about the development of "Affluent Attitude," when "people with middle-class incomes now have the expectations that were once reserved for the rich," such as spas, designer toasters, and name-brand clothing.[9]

But beware of moralizing! At the same time, there are good reasons—spiritual bases—to feel a certain kind of entitlement. If we are entitled to anything, it is because we are human beings who—by simply being alive—image the incomprehensible God. We thus should have no shame in saying we deserve healthful food, safe quarter, education, provision for a future, fair treatment in work. All of these pertain to the divine enfoldment and vocation of every human life. But it is precisely these goods that are deserved by all human beings, not just Western ones.

So entitlement today does have a worthy basis: an innate sense that we should be at peace and even flourish. But in addition to the zest for fulfillment that springs from our createdness, many of us have learned unrealistic expectations about what we deserve. These expectations deprive others around the world of what they deserve to be human. These inflated expectations are what we can truly call "entitlement."

Thus, one of the most dangerous and important questions to pose today in the public square is a question both economic and spiritual: Of what are *all* God's children truly deserving?

When God *is* brought into the picture, part of our culture of entitlement is often thinking that we must have money, substantial money, before we can fully do God's will. Some bestselling books today make precisely this case. Who wouldn't like to do discipleship from the back seat of a limousine, or be overwhelmed with a choice between which charity should get your thousands of dollars of beneficence this year?

Karl Rahner warned against theology becoming the "underpinning of a life of middle-class ethics supervised by God."[10] Ignatius, who once knew high society but also knew extreme poverty, remarked that some people want to have certain benefits, and then to serve God with those benefits. But that way of thinking about our spiritual lives confuses the ends with the means. It makes serving God the means to the end of accumulating wealth. This is a good example of a broken desire, like a bent arrow traveling off course. Ignatius says that people who want this "desire God to come to their disordered affections," instead of directing their affections to God.[11] Part of a spiritual response to entitlement is asking ourselves whether we are confusing ends and means.

By layers, we may shed our entitled selves. True releasement from the entitled self is a self more intimate with God, both more confident and more loosely held, more centered (in God's personal devotion to one's dignity) and decentered (in realizing God shows the same devotion to all people around the globe). Levinas described something like this when he considered the "trauma of a fission of the self that occurs in an adventure undergone with God or through God."[12]

KNOWING AND BEING KNOWN

There is an authentic spiritual impulse at the heart of our branding economy. We use brands to do identity work for us, finally, out of a desire to be recognized by others, by a power greater than ourselves; and the desire to recognize and know others, to commune with others under a power greater than ourselves. And in this recognizing and being recognized, we experience that greater power that draws us inward and outward.

And so our brand economy discloses a task for spiritual maturity: knowing and being known by ourselves and others, without being governed by entitlement regarding who we are or what we buy.

We can't do without "stuff." There is nothing wrong with buying, nothing wrong with the existence of brands. In order to turn the spiritual corner before us, we will need to integrate who we are with what we buy. To realize that we each have some freedom to accept God's gifting us with life, by becoming someone who stewards more life for others. In that work, God's gift of life becomes more believable to others, and awareness of and responsible relationship to God spreads through our use of our resources, through consciousness about those affected by our purchases.

We live out our relation to our ultimate meaning through what and how we buy. Let the integration of faith and economy be the mark of the true spiritual seeker today, a consuming faith.

A CONSUMING FAITH

A consuming faith, that is, a faith that increasingly overspreads every domain of being and knowing, is one that constantly questions uncritical faith in consumption.

A consuming faith does not allow itself to be restricted to good intentions, holy thoughts, or spiritual words. Such a faith slowly, unevenly, and with many reversals influences the practices of purchasing as much as the fealties of friendship, the buying of brands as much as fidelity of family.

Faith is only faith if it is allowed to flower into the many networks of our relationships—economic, religious, erotic. A consuming faith not only increases spiritual maturity about branding culture . . . it also carries us beyond the brands of religion and spirituality to which we entrusted ourselves at earlier stages of faith. The brand of faith that we think explains everything must itself become the kindling to be consumed by an enlarged capacity for following God in ever-deeper dimensions of our relationships.

A consuming faith is painful gift and blessed task, precisely because it will consume our past beliefs and practices.

ON READING SCRIPTURE

The one precondition for reading the Bible fruitfully is knowing how to read it.

I long ago gave up the idea that the Bible has one answer for anything. I confess to nausea at any mention of "a biblical worldview," which has for many years now seemed to me like something between intellectual dishonesty and spiritual manipulation.

The Bible is a motley assortment of stories, poems, myths, hymns, letters, histories, and aphorisms that submit to no single controlling principle. Despite all attempts to smooth over the tensions, discrepancies, and contradictions in it, the heterogeneity of the Bible defies all attempts to reduce it to one program, theology, perspective, or worldview. Even calling it "the Bible" (literally, "the book") can be the beginning of idolatry. (I much prefer "scriptures," literally "writings.") Christians have continually attempted to make this human book docetically divine. But accepting its thoroughgoing humanity is the only honest way to attune oneself to its divine and revelatory character. We are still so in thrall to Enlightenment thinking and the history of Western rationality that we presume that being honest with ourselves about the Bible's inconsistencies, ambiguities, and contradictions in some way impugns its spiritual power. Such presumption only convicts our attempts to confuse it with God.

A critical releasement to scripture is, for me, the only way to make sense of it as an educated person today. What I mean by "releasement" is allowing oneself to be caught up in scriptures' tensions, ambiguities, slips, cracks, demands, charges, directions, guidelines, overtones, seductions, rhetorics, legerdemain, crevices, banalities, interruptions, exhortations, assertions, reversals, and obscurities. To say to the text, "Let it be with me according to your word" (Luke 1:38).

This is, after all, the way human communication works. How could we hear a word from scripture if it did not speak our language, the language of stutters, persuasions, arguments, incompleteness, vagueness, and allusiveness? God never communicates anything except according to the mode of the receiver, said Aquinas, and our mode is first and last human.

But this releasement to the human hands of scripture is not all; we must be "critical." By critical I do not necessarily mean contrarian or negative. I mean that when we come to the scriptures, we always do so in a highly particular way. We always come as *ourselves*, with our own personal and communal histories, with our questions from our time, with our anxieties and answers, with our assumptions and attitudes. To say to the text, "Come now, let us argue it out" (Isaiah 1:18). Sometimes what we bring to scripture has already been influenced by scripture—whether through prayer or study of it, through its influence on our culture, or its influence on those who have influenced us. With all that we bring, we have to be ready to be critical with scripture, to question, wonder about, ponder, suspect, and even at times reject what we find there, remembering that what we find there is always in part a projection of ourselves onto those letters, spaces, and punctuations. (Which means what we reject now we should always reserve the humility to reconsider at a later stage of our lives.)

All of this makes dealing with the Bible sometimes messy, unpredictable, uncomfortable, and murky. Anything else is pious overcertainty or adolescent refusal. But we cannot permanently refuse to trust texts. All of us can and do, will and must, pitch ourselves into the worlds of some text in which we invest ourselves and hope for direction. That text could be a record, a person, a repair manual, a book of poetry, a birth certificate, a website, a tome of philosophy, a celebrity's sayings, one's own internal dialogue, or the Bible—or, more commonly, some combination of all those texts.

Notes

CHAPTER 1

1. The Conference Board, "Managing the Corporate Brand," Research Report 1214-98-RR, 1998, p. 16.

2. Ibid., p. 24.

3. Al Ries and Laura Ries, *The 22 Immutable Laws of Branding* (New York: HarperCollins, 1998), p. 58.

4. The Conference Board, p. 27.

5. David Carr, "Coming Late, Fashionably, Teen Vogue Joins a Crowd," *The New York Times*, 13 January 2003, p. C10.

6. Alissa Quart, *Branded* (Perseus, 2003), p. 53.

7. Naomi Klein, *No Logo* (New York: Picador, 1999), p. 66.

8. Ruth La Ferla, "Boys to Men: Fashion Pack Turns Younger," *New York Times*, 14 July 2002, section 9, pp. 1, 6.

9. Mark C. Taylor, *Disfiguring: Art, Architecture, Religion* (Chicago: University of Chicago, 1992), p. 188.

10. Chip Walker, "Can TV Save the Planet?" *American Demographics*, May 1996, p. 42, in Klein, pp. 119–120.

11. Klein, pp. 120–121.

12. Cris Prystay and Montira Narkvichien, "'Sex and the City' Is a Hit in Asia," *Wall Street Journal*, 9 August 2002, p. B2.

13. Waters, *Globalization*, 2nd edition (New York: Routledge, 2001), p. 63.

14. Roland Robertson in ibid., p. 4.

15. Dean Hoge et al., *Young Adult Catholics* (Notre Dame, IN: University of Notre Dame Press, 2001).

16. Sharon Parks, *Big Questions, Worthy Dreams: Mentoring Young Adults in their Search for Meaning* (San Francisco: Jossey-Bass, 2000), pp. 207ff.

17. Ibid., p. 187.

CHAPTER 2

1. "The Didache," in Cyril Richardson (ed.), *Early Christian Fathers* (Macmillan, 1970), p. 171.

CHAPTER 3

1. Robert Schreiter, *The New Catholicity: Theology Between the Global and the Local* (Maryknoll, NY: Orbis, 1997), p. 113.

2. Karl Rahner, "Morality Without Moralizing," in Karl Lehmann, Albert Raffelt, and Harvey D. Egan (eds.), *The Content of Faith: The Best of Karl Rahner's Theological Writings* (New York: Crossroad, 1994), pp. 537, 539–540.

3. Karl Rahner interview with Hans Georg Koch and David A. Seeber, "The Church in a Secularized Society," in Paul Imhof and Hubert Biallowons (eds.), *Karl Rahner in Dialogue* (New York: Crossroad, 1986), trans. Donald W. Reck, p. 167.

4. The Conference Board, "Managing the Corporate Brand," Research Report 1214-98-RR, 1998, p. 20.

5. "General Introduction," in George E. Ganss (ed.), *Ignatius of Loyola: Spiritual Exercises and Selected Works* (New York: Paulist, 1991), p. 58.

6. "The Autobiography," #99, in *Ignatius of Loyola*.

7. Cited in Maria Harris, *Teaching and Religious Imagination* (San Francisco: Harper and Row, 1987).

8. "The Spiritual Exercises," #47 in *Ignatius of Loyola*.

9. Ibid., #192.

10. Ibid., ##137–146.

11. Ibid., #54.

12. Ibid., #109.

13. Ibid., #53.

14. Susan Fournier and Michael Guiry, "An Emerald Green Jaguar," in Leigh McAlister and Michael L. Rothschild (eds.), *Advances in Consumer Research* (20:352–358) (Provo, Utah: Association for Consumer Research), pp. 355–357. I am indebted for this reference and to the following references to Caughey and Belk to the very helpful work of economist Juliet Schor, who originally inspired my approach to this chapter with her book *The Overspent American* (New York: Basic Books, 1998), which it seemed to me could be productively "reframed" theologically.

15. Caughey, *Imaginary Social Worlds: A Cultural Approach* (Lincoln: University of Nebraska Press, 1984), p. 185.

16. Ibid., p. 176.

17. Robert H. Nelson, *Economics as Religion* (University Park, PA: Pennsylvania State University Press), p. 326.

18. Colin Campbell in Nelson, *Economics as Religion*, pp. 325–326.

19. Russell Belk, "Possessions and the Extended Self," *Journal of Consumer Research* 15 (September) 1988, p.139.

20. Quart, *Branded*, p. 89.

21. "The Spiritual Exercises," #365.

22. Chuck Klosterman, *Fargo Rock City* (New York: Scribner, 2001), p. 263, quoting Fieldy of the band Korn.

23. Howard Schultz, *Pour Your Heart into It* (New York: Hyperion, 1997), p. 5.

24. Friedrich Schleiermacher, *The Christian Faith*, H.R. Mackintosh and J.S. Stewart (eds.) (Edinburgh: T&T Clark, 1989 [1830]), p. 12.

25. The Conference Board, p. 12.

26. Quart, *Branded*, p. 35.

27. Klein, *No Logo*, p. 56.

28. Alan Cowell, "Bumpy Start for De Beers's Retail Diamond Venture," *New York Times*, 21 November 2002, pp. W1, W7.

29. "The Spiritual Exercises," ##169ff.

30. Quart, p. 18.

31. Chris Jenkins, "Sponsors Make NASCAR's Wheels Go 'Round," *USA Today*, 12 July 2002 (www.usatoday.com).

CHAPTER 4

1. These testimonies were accessed at the National Labor Committee website: www.nlcnet.org. I am grateful to the NLC for their tireless and pioneering work in publicizing the labor practices of global American corporations.

2. Fred Dickey, "Levi Strauss and the Price We Pay," *Los Angeles Times Magazine*, 1 December 2002 (www.latimes.com).

3. Naomi Klein, *No Logo* (New York: Picador, 1999), p. 221.

4. Ibid., p. 214.

5. Ibid., p. 4.

6. Ibid., p. 22. See the interesting example of this regarding Tommy Hilfiger in *No Logo*, p. 24.

7. Ibid., p. 196.

8. Ibid., p. 68.

9. See, for example, Luke 4:30, John 4:31–32, 8:59, and 20:19 and Mark 6:48.

10. See, for example, Luke 24:36–43 and John 20:24–29. See also 1 John 4:1–3, 2 John 7, and Col 2:8f.

11. See Dean Hoge, William Dinges, Mary Johnson, and Juan Gonzales Jr., *Young Adult Catholics: Religion in the Culture of Choice* (Notre Dame, IN: University of Notre Dame Press, 2001).

12. Klein, *No Logo*, p. 195.

13. The Conference Board, "Managing the Corporate Brand," Research Report 1214-98-RR, 1998, p. 22.

14. Jeffrey F. Rayport, "Introduction," in David E. Carter, *Branding: The Power of Market Identity* (New York: Hearst Books International, 1999), p. 4.

CHAPTER 5

1. See, for example, Romans 12, 1 Corinthians 6:12ff, 1 Corinthians 10:16–17, and 1 Corinthians 12:12–31.

2. Drew Leder, *The Absent Body* (Chicago: University of Chicago Press, 1990), p. 19.

3. Ibid., p. 29.

4. See ibid., pp. 36–68.

5. Ibid., p. 66.

6. Ibid., italics mine.

7. Ibid., pp. 67–68.

8. Ibid., p. 68, italics mine.

9. Ibid.

10. Ibid.

11. Ibid., p. 160.

12. Emmanuel Levinas, "Substitution," in Seán Hand (ed.), *The Levinas Reader* (Cambridge, MA: Blackwell, 1996), p. 104.

13. Levinas, "Ethics as First Philosophy," in *The Levinas Reader*, p. 81.

CHAPTER 6

1. Marc Lacey, "Via Hollywood, A Glimpse of African Poverty," *New York Times*, 21 December 2002, pp. A1, A22.

2. Katherine Marsh, "Spring Break in Managua," *Rolling Stone* 852 (October 26, 2000), p. 90.

3. Radiohead, *Kid A* (Capitol, 2000)

4. Naomi Klein, *No Logo* (New York: Picador, 1999), pp. 60–61.

5. "The Autobiography," #88, in George E. Ganss (ed.), *Ignatius of Loyola: Spiritual Exercises and Selected Works* (New York: Paulist, 1991).

6. Richard W. Stevenson and Richard A. Oppel Jr., "Fed Chief Blames Corporate Greed," *New York Times*, 17 July 2002, p. A1.

7. Drew Leder, *The Absent Body* (Chicago: University of Chicago Press, 1990), p. 117, italics mine.

8. Alissa Quart, *Branded: The Buying and Selling of Teenagers* (Cambridge, MA: Perseus, 2003), p. 71.

9. David Brooks, "Affluent Attitude," *New York Times*, 28 December 2002, p. A15.

10. Karl Rahner, "A Courageous Worldwide Theology," in *National Jesuit News*, vol. 8, June 1979, p. 10, cited in Richard McBrien, *Catholicism* (San Francisco: HarperSanFrancisco, 1994), p. 1212.

11. "The Spiritual Exercises," #169, in *Ignatius of Loyola*.

12. Levinas, "God and Philosophy," in Seán Hand (ed.), *The Levinas Reader* (Cambridge, MA: Blackwell, 1996), p. 186.

About the Author

Tom Beaudoin's work seeks to develop a theology of everyday life that is animated by the search for how we know God in freeing each other. He is a visiting assistant professor of theology at Boston College and the author of *Virtual Faith: The Irreverent Spiritual Quest of Generation X*, as well as many articles on theology and culture.

His lectures on spirituality and economics have been published in Catholic and Protestant contexts: as monographs by Santa Clara University and Princeton Theological Seminary, and in the journals *Currents in Theology and Mission* and *Lutheran Education*.

His forthcoming projects focus on the development of a contemporary practical theology through appropriation of the work of philosopher Michel Foucault.

He is a bass player in the rock band Incizion and lives with his spouse, Martina Verba, a psychotherapist, in Brookline, Massachusetts.